Understanding

Friends

Alistair Ross is a Baptist Minister in Bexleyheath, Kent. An experienced counsellor, he has also worked in a psychiatric hospital running group therapy. He is a Visiting Lecturer at Spurgeons College on pastoral theology, pastoral care and counselling, and is married with two young children.

UNDERSTANDING FRIENDS

*Getting the Best
Out of Friendship*

ALISTAIR ROSS

Triangle

First published 1993
Triangle
SPCK
Holy Trinity Church
Marylebone Road
London NW1 4DU

Copyright © 1993 Alistair Ross

All rights reserved. No part of this book may
be reproduced or transmitted in any form or by
any means, electronic or mechanical, including
photocopying, recording, or by any information
storage and retrieval system, without permission
in writing from the publisher.

British Library Cataloguing in Publication Data
A catalogue record for this book is available from the British Library.
ISBN 0–281–04694–8

Typeset by Inforum, Rowlands Castle, Hants
Printed and bound in Great Britain by
BPCC Paperbacks Ltd
Member of BPCC Ltd

Contents

	Foreword by David Atkinson	vii
	Acknowledgements	xi
1	An endangered species	1
2	The origin of friendship	14
3	Making friends	27
4	Making friends with ourselves	48
5	When friendships fail	68
6	Obstacles to friendship	79
7	The transforming friendship	91
	Notes	101

Foreword

According to Emerson, 'A friend may well be reckoned the masterpiece of nature.' Everyone, he says, searches for friends. We know how precious a good friendship can be, how sad it is for someone to be friendless.

Yet if this is such an important part of being human, it is very surprising how little friendship seems to feature in contemporary Christian thinking. I turned up several dictionaries of theology and of Christian ethics, and although there are plenty of entries on love, and on sex, there are very few on 'friends'.

This is perplexing in the light of the way the Fourth Gospel speaks of Jesus's relation to his disciples: 'I have called you friends.' The word for friend is closely related to the way St John speaks about love and is contrasted with slavery: 'I have not called you servants, but I have called you friends.' Just as some of the rabbis spoke about Jews being 'friends of God', so Jesus speaks of disciples as his friends, taken into his confidence, trusting his word, respecting his will, finding in their mutual friendship a response to the love of God. There is a liberty, an intimacy, a mysteriously transcendent and loving quality to friendship. It is most often in friendship relationships to others that we discover who we are in ourselves.

So why is friendship becoming what Alistair Ross, in this valuable book, calls 'an endangered species'?

Is it that our highly individualized culture, with its inheritance from the Enlightenment, has got caught up in

Understanding friends

technological ways of thinking which see human beings as technicians, interveners in the system, problem-solvers? Everything, even other people, becomes subject to our will, our control, our technique. This crowds out more personal ways of living, and the result is alienation. We become alienated from one another and from our environment. We become divided up within ourselves. And down these deep fissures which open up in our culture go words like 'community' and 'friendship'. Is it that friendship gets lost in a culture which either turns love into sentimentality, or else reduces love to sex and then sees sex as really just a matter of technique? Friendship disappears in a culture that does not take time to make friends.

Sometimes this happens at home. We may share the same house and the same television set, but there need be little mutuality, sharing or intimacy. Sometimes the setting is our place of work. The workplace can become merely the factory. This may be literally so, or the 'factory' may be the church or the school, and then the product is the worshipper in the pew or the child being processed to fit society's expectations. Or we may invest too much in work, the duty of work, the demands of work, the affirmation we receive from work, so that work takes all our attention. That might be another reason why friendships are a scarce commodity.

Sometimes the setting is church itself. We have a long tradition of upholding the values of marriage and family, which, in the Western world, at least since the Industrial Revolution, has been understood mostly as the nuclear family. And the church arranges much of its life around these institutions. We have rituals to help us in marriage and family life. We organize occasions, parties, celebrations, for weddings and baptisms. We put time and attention into family worship. But the vast majority of our population do

Foreword

not live in the nuclear family pattern. As a church we don't say much to that majority. We lack similar rituals to support friendships. Friendship gets lost from our vocabulary. The heavy timetable of church meetings and committees can, for some often unexamined reason, absorb so much Christian attention that we don't have time for friends.

How very good, therefore, that Alistair Ross has brought us back to the importance of friendship. As a pastoral theologian, counsellor, and minister in a local church, he is well qualified to recognize the difficulties we get ourselves into by missing out on this dimension in Christian thought and Christian life. He has worked with people in difficulties. Drawing on his knowledge both of theology and of pastoral psychology, he understands how we think and behave. He writes in a warm, caring and practical way. He shows us how we can learn again to make friends, and indicates the things that get in the way of friendship. He points us eventually to Jesus in whose service we can discover that he calls even us his friends.

I believe this book will be very helpful to many of us. I am pleased to have this opportunity to commend it.

David Atkinson
January 1993

Acknowledgements

There are many people I would like to thank, who have helped me produce this book, and who have shown me particular friendship over the years. Many thanks are due to Rosie Nixson, who has edited my last two books and helped me with this one. She has helped me learn how to write, though I still do not understand split infinitives! Thanks also to Pat Bradley, who wore out several red pens in refining a rough manuscript into a book. I also want to thank David Atkinson for writing the foreword and for his patient encouragement and supervision, as I have struggled to complete a research degree.

I have learnt that the people who have been particular friends to me are those people who have believed in 'me', and in all that I have struggled to be and to do. Thanks then to Peter, Malcolm and Myra's group, Jeannie, Keith, Andy and Jonathan.

I also want to express a special sense of gratitude to my close friend Mike, who means a tremendous amount to me. Last, but not least, is my wife Judy and our children Hannah and Toby.

1

An endangered species

I stood at the door of our house, watching Hannah, my four-year-old daughter, marching off to her new infant school, proudly wearing her first school uniform. She seemed such a small person to be launched on her own into a big and not always friendly world. I wondered who she would play with. I wanted her to make friends and be happy. I couldn't fight her battles in the playground: from now on it was down to her. 'How on earth', I thought to myself, 'can a four-year-old cope with all these things?' At the end of her first full day I asked what she had done at lunchtime. A lump came into my throat when Hannah said that she had sat all on her own to eat her sandwiches. Each day Judy and I would try to piece together how school was going from the fragments of information that she gave us. At the end of the week our normal parental anxiety subsided when she told us the names of her friends and announced, 'We don't play with boys'. That will change soon enough!

Looking at life through the eyes of a child made us realize what a vital part friends play in our development as individuals, and in our enjoyment of life. It has made me think about my friends and how important they are to me. One particular friend and I were discussing recently how we had influenced each other over the past twelve years. Mike ended by saying that he felt my influence in his life has

Understanding friends

been 'deeply rooted'. My response to that was that I felt very proud to be 'deeply rooted' with him. It was quite an intimate conversation. As I look around I can see that there is a crying need for intimacy, the intimacy of knowing that we have been accepted and understood by some other human being. Men find this particularly difficult to do and although this book has not been written exclusively for men, it does reflect my masculine struggles for intimacy and acceptance in friendship. I do hope that men especially will discover a new sense of intimacy as a result. To know that there is someone to whom we matter and are important enables us to live and enjoy life in a better way. However, there is a problem. Where and how do we find friends?

One way to begin is by deciding what we are looking for. We are like pirates on a desert island, digging with the hope of discovering buried treasure, and it helps if we have a map, on which X marks the spot. What are the clues that tell us whether we are digging for our friends in the right place?

One thing we look for in a friend is that he or she should be someone who accepts us. When I went to university I moved into student accommodation where I had been allocated a bedroom and had to share a bathroom and kitchen with twelve others. To combat the loneliness I felt as a result of leaving home and living in a new place, I hoped to make friends with the people I lived with. Within two days I was forced to discard that hope like a screwed up piece of litter. My room was on a floor where most of the students were in their second year and had already become friends. They made it very clear that if I wanted to be friends with them I would have to join in all-night drinking, water fights and setting off fire extinguishers. My biggest disappointment was that they were not willing to accept me as 'me'.

An endangered species

They would be friends only if I was prepared to be like them.

Do you ever get the feeling that much of life is spent 'fitting-in'? We try so hard to be acceptable to other people: our family, those we meet at college, the people we work with, our neighbours, and even those we worship with. Friends are people who accept us as we are, whether we conform or not. Frequently when I am counselling, people tell me about parents who showed little physical or emotional signs of approval. Such parental attitudes leave scars, because they make a child think that love has to be earned by perfection. Friends are people who accept us, whatever we may or may not achieve.

Another clue about friends is that they are people who like us. Do you remember those teenage years when you could spend hours in the bathroom examining your face in minute detail, wishing your hair was blonde and curly instead of straight and mousey brown, and wondering what you could do about the bags under your eyes? Then, horror of all horrors, the spot. Always in a prominent position and always on the day when you most wanted to impress someone of the opposite sex. And do you also remember that euphoric feeling when you found out that someone did actually want to go out with you? It was like walking on cloud nine. Life was worth living after all.

It still feels good when someone lets us know that they like us, even when we are no longer insecure adolescents, but fully mature adults. There is still part of me that feels great when I discover that someone likes me. I remember Roy with whom I worked for two years, running self-awareness groups at a theological college. I felt happy when he said that he would miss working with me. Was that because I was a brilliant group facilitator? No, Roy was much more

Understanding friends

experienced than I was. But I felt I mattered to him, even though this one group was all we had in common.

Friendships, for men especially, often evolve out of common interests. Doing together things which we enjoy—seeing the latest film, playing in the same rugby or football team, going to evening classes or to the mums' and toddlers' group—can become a springboard for involvement in another person's life. The time comes when that person communicates that he or she is interested in us. Knowing that someone likes us, and will miss us if we don't turn up or can't make an event, is deeply affirming and does something special to us. It is like swapping your battered Ford for a Ferrari, like being a walkman that gets a new set of long-life batteries, like thinking you are going for a meal at McDonalds and ending up at the Ritz.

A friend is also someone who is loyal. Friends stand up for us in our absence and stay with us through the ups and downs of our life, just as we stay with them through the ups and downs of theirs. This is not always an easy task, as a recent holiday experience reminded me.

Our family was at the seaside with my brother and his family. The children went on all the usual train rides, slides and merry-go-rounds but my brother and I dared each other to go on a fairground ride called the 'Octopus'. We were clamped into our seat and this machine proceeded to rotate and undulate at an incredible speed. I looked across at him and said, 'Whose stupid idea was this?' At last it began to slow down and our bodies felt as though they were attached to our stomachs once more. Then came the dreadful realization that it was all going to happen again backwards. After what seemed an eternity we stopped, and felt the security of standing on solid ground. Both of us promised not to do anything so silly again. Staying friends often requires us to

An endangered species

hang on like this even when we feel we may both be going off the rails.

All friendships go through difficult times when it feels hard to hang onto one's friend. There are times when we just don't want to be bothered with another person's problems as we have enough of our own. But such times can produce a degree of loyalty that actually enhances the relationship. Knowing that your friend is going to stick with you when it seems that everything else has fallen apart is like being thrown a lifebelt when you are drowning.

Above all, perhaps, friends are people who express affection or love. Phil Collins, the rock musician said at a concert:

> Everybody, everywhere
> needs someone to love,
> someone to hug,
> someone to kiss,
> someone to miss.

Friends are people whom we love and can hug, whom we can kiss and will miss. C.S. Lewis, drawing on his vast knowledge of literature, wrote: 'To the Ancients, friendship seemed the happiest and most fully human of all loves; the crown of life . . . . This alone, of all the loves, seemed to raise you to the level of gods or angels.'[1] Friends love us as we are and stick with us when life becomes tough; that is why we like and love them so much.

Do you have friends like that? I hope so. But they are rare: friends are an endangered species. There are plenty of 'acquaintances' around and in the current fragmented social and cultural habitat they are easier to find than real friends. This raises a whole string of questions. Are friends really important nowadays? If not, who is to blame for this tragic

Understanding friends

situation? Is it really as bad as all that? The author John Mortimer touches on some of these questions in a review of *The Oxford Book of Friendship*:

> It makes you think hard about your friends and even to wonder if, in this sexy, egotistic, and competitive world of ours, the whole business that meant so much to David and Jonathan . . . has not now gone somewhat out of style.[2]

The answers to such questions take us to the very foundations of our society. Why is it that friendship, a foundational part of one's life, seems now to be under threat from some forces that shape society?

Foundations are especially important, because if they are unstable then all that is built on them will be unstable too. I live in a charming, old-world style bungalow, on a small but secluded piece of land on the edge of London, surrounded by trees. It is a tranquil place to live. From my study window I can watch fox cubs playing on the lawn, squirrels jumping from tree to tree, and an endless variety of birds like jays and magpies. Once we even had a buzzard in our garden—but that is another story. However, there is a major problem that no-one would ever guess: the bungalow is 23 centimetres lower in one corner than in all the others. There is a large tree about four metres from the house and over the years its roots have spread and begun to extract all the moisture from the soil. Slowly but surely over a twenty-year period the earth on which the foundations were built began to shrink and the corner of the house went with it. One day close inspection of one room revealed a crack running diagonally from floor to ceiling. Our foundations had been sinking for years but we only noticed when we found a crack on the surface.

An endangered species

Let me suggest a number of areas in which our society's foundations cause problems when it comes to making friends and developing friendships.

SELFISHNESS
We live in a selfish world. I dread every Saturday morning during November and December, because this is when anyone who has children is inundated with requests for the latest toy which has just been advertised. Every Saturday, Hannah will explain in great detail why she must have such and such a toy and what amazing things it can do. Advertisers have learned to convince us that anything we 'want' can be translated into something we 'need', which in turn is translated into something we cannot live without. This goes on all around us twenty-four hours a day and it becomes absorbed, almost unconsciously, into our thinking. A Christian sociologist has summed it up in the title of his book, *Need: The New Religion*.

The next time you go shopping in a store containing toys or sweets, be prepared for the following experience. It begins with a loud child's voice, 'I want . . .', to which a parent replies, 'No'. Then the cajoling and wheedling begins: 'I promise I'll be good . . . I'll pay you back . . . Just this once . . . If you love me . . . Why have they (older brothers or sisters) got one and not me?' This is soon followed by crying and screaming, and if the child is desperate enough it will throw itself on the floor! Often the embarrassed parent gives in just to keep the child quiet. An adult might think, 'What a little horror', but for the child this is a matter of life and death. He or she has a desire, a need—and it must be met.

A four-year-old boy was swimming in the local pool. A man who had been doing a number of lengths cursed and

Understanding friends

swore when the boy momentarily got in his way. When the boy's parents took issue with him he told them that he had a busy job and went there to relax and did not want it ruined by some kid getting in his way. His anger was so great that he threatened to 'smash their faces in'. He was so intent on getting his 'needs' met that he had become selfish. The trouble is that friends have needs too: they make demands, they expect something from us. If we are consumed by what we think is the vital task of having our needs met, we fail to notice and respond to the needs of others. When that happens we may never know what real friends are.

MATERIALISM
We live in a material world. Madonna, a rock singer who loves to shock with her sexually explicit performances, videos and books, has produced some profound songs. She also reflects the culture we live in, and one of her best-selling records is called 'Material World'. We live in a world that worships money, where everyone and everything seems to have a price. Money holds out the promise that there is no limit to the fulfilment of human desires. Harrod's, the world-famous London store and mecca for tourists, prides itself on being able to meet its customers' demands, and even managed on one occasion to produce an elephant. But even Harrod's cannot provide friends. You cannot buy friends.

We want people to like us and accept us, and it is easy in a status-conscious society to fall into the trap of thinking that our value can be measured in terms of what we possess. In most of us there is a desire for belonging and approval and in a material world many seem to think this can be bought like any other commodity. We are so busy making money to buy things which will impress others, and give us

An endangered species

social standing and respect, that we have no time left for friends. Little wonder if we find life empty and unsatisfying in those rare moments when we get off the treadmill of our lives. So often we need friends to help us to be honest about our lives and in a material world there is not much room for them. All of us have a hunger for relationships and friends that needs to be met, and money doesn't meet it. Jesus told a story about a young man with lots of money who left home in search of excitement. While he had money he had friends, but as soon as the money ran out so did the friends (Luke 15.11–32).

THROW IT AWAY
Our material world is also a throw-away world. Some advertisers are blatant about their aim of training children to think in materialistic ways. If they can implant the idea that the latest is the best, then any object or fashion can become out of date within a year.

This was brought home to me when I decided to buy a CD-player. The manager of the hi-fi shop showed me the special offer he was having on one of last year's models and explained that it was mechanically the same machine as one with a new front which cost a great deal more. He told me that in Tokyo it was not unknown for Westerners to go to the rubbish dump and help themselves to fully working electrical goods which had been dumped because they were last year's models and no longer fashionable. It is the same with our acquaintances: those we have today may not be fashionable tomorrow. Similarly, we may be tempted to choose 'friends' who are good to be seen with, only to drop them later for a new 'in-crowd'.

This obsolescence affects us in other ways as well. I dream of a world where you can get a toaster that produces

Understanding friends

nice lightly toasted bread instead of burning the slice to a cinder. At present I feel like throwing our existing toaster away and getting a new one. Why? Because I have to stand over it while my bread is in it, to prevent the slice turning to charcoal. If something doesn't do what we want it to do or becomes inconvenient, it's easiest to throw it away. Friends are sometimes inconvenient like this, and they don't always do what we want them to—so should we start the search for a 'better' model? In a world where manufacturers build a limited working life into their products, we have lost the art of maintenance. We no longer need to make weekly checks and oil a part here or tighten a screw there. Similarly we can forget to maintain a friendship, and neglect to make those adjustments which keep it in a finely tuned state.

Another aspect of this throw-away world, where time, patience and repair have little value, is its focus on the 'instant'. In our house tea-making is still considered an art. The water is boiled, the tea-pot is warmed, the water is reboiled and poured over two spoonfuls of Assam tea. This is left to brew for four minutes before the tea is strained and put into a china cup. There's nothing instant about it. Yet the fast food world we live in is always wanting things done in a hurry. Like everyone else we live with the tyranny of the urgent.

Friendships may start in an instant, but they need time, effort and attention if they are to grow, and this goes against the grain of modern living.

FRAGMENTED LIVES
We also live in a fragmented world, as a girl called Mary found out. Mary had moved away from her family in Scotland when she married her husband, John. Now living in

An endangered species

Surrey and seven months pregnant, Mary went into premature labour. Unable to get hold of her husband, she called on her next-door neighbour, who had always kept herself to herself. The neighbour answered the door to find a young, frightened Scots lass standing there. Mary explained that she thought she had gone into labour but never having experienced anything like it before, she wasn't sure. As her neighbour had two children Mary thought she might be able to help. The neighbour explained politely that she didn't want to get involved, suggested that she call the emergency services and shut the door, leaving Mary standing there. Mary felt desperate and alone, wishing she were back home. She badly needed a friend.

As an increasing number of people move away from home and family to find work, as companies relocate, and as promotion often involves a change of area, more and more people are uprooted. That uprooting often means that friends are left behind and despite considerable effort, it becomes almost impossible to maintain those friendships. When people are in need there is no longer the supportive network of family and friends to help. An awful consequence of Britain's divorce rate (the second highest in Europe) is the increasing number of strained and distant family relationships. Family life seems to be falling to pieces. A single mother who comes to our mums and new babies group, said that other than her health visitor, the mothers she met there were the only people she saw each week.

Her experience helps to show how we live in a depersonalized world. Sandra works for the Samaritans, an organization that gives help in crisis situations, through a twenty-four hour telephone service, 365 days a year. She discovered that there were regular callers whose lives were not in

Understanding friends

imminent crisis, but who rang up just because they wanted to hear another human voice. Each person needs to feel that they are of worth and value, not just some anonymous item in a computer databank. The more we can do from the comfort of our own home, communicating via telephone or even by means of a computer terminal, the more we become marooned and depersonalized as people. All too easily we find we are no longer a name, simply a credit card number. Jeffrey Masson reflects on this process as he recounts a search for himself which took him into and out of psychoanalysis.

> Psychoanalysis . . . cannot transform the tumultuous storm of human relationships into the artificial calm of therapeutic alliance . . . . What I was searching for, and what psychoanalysis promises, cannot in fact, be given by another person, cannot be found in a theory, or a profession, no matter how well-meaning. It is only, I am convinced, to be had, or not had, through living. There are no experts in loving, no scholars of living, no doctors of the human emotions and no gurus of the soul. But we need not be alone; friendship is a precious gift.[3]

Just as there now seem to be so many factors that fragment the society in which we live, making the process of making friends more difficult, so there is also an increasing recognition of the value and importance of friends.

If 'God is friendship' as Aelred, a twelfth-century monk suggested,[4] where does God actually fit into this process of making friends? If the world was meant to be a good place (as the book of Genesis declares), where people could experience love, security and acceptance, expressed in trusting relationships, why has it become so lonely, fragmented and depersonalized? God's answers to these questions of frag-

An endangered species

mented relationships and the search for genuine and understanding friends, centre on his son.

Remember those sinking foundations of my bungalow? Although it had become cracked and flawed, because of its setting and character the problem was worth solving. The whole house needed to be underpinned. For six weeks, three men with small pneumatic drills dug out the foundations and replaced them with tons of concrete. Unfortunately we were still living in the house at the time. Yet the end result was worth all the time, effort, money, noise, filth and inconvenience. In the same way, God thought the world worth so much that no expense was spared in repairing its broken foundations. God's son Jesus came to live in this lonely, fragmented and selfish world. He showed people what true friendship with God is like and how it can be part of our experience. No more were our lives to be cracked and in danger of collapse. The cost was immense. The perfect man and perfect God died for imperfect men and women on an imperfect, wooden cross. On his bruised and bleeding shoulders he carried all the muck and imperfection of the world, past, present and future. Why did Jesus do this? He gave this reason to his friends the disciples, and John recorded it for us: 'Greater love has no-one than this, that one lay down his life for his friends' (John 15.13).

Jesus, his death, his coming back to life and his return to heaven where he now rules, is the message to be taken throughout the world, so that the whole human race can be friends with God once more. For twenty centuries the Church has taught this and lived it. This message was first entrusted to Jesus's friends. As we look at friendship in this book, we will discover that friends play a vital part in recreating the world as God wants it to be and in the enjoyment of living in this world as God wants us to live.

2

The origin of friendship

Finding friends is big business. Dating agencies, lonely hearts clubs, introduction agencies and friendship bureaux use emotionally loaded slogans like 'Why be Lonely?', 'Stuck in a rut? And no-one really special?' to tug at one's heart. Their aim is to attract customers who will pay to be introduced to someone else in the hope of friendship and often marriage. The personal columns of newspapers with their small ads do much the same:

> MEN, why always slim ladies wanted? Why not a sincere 34-year old fun-loving person with a bit more. Busy workwise but will make time for Mr Right. Photo please.

There is something in us that finds friendship an almost indispensable part of life. Why is this? Why do we want friends? This chapter is going to explore some of these questions and suggest some answers.

Thinking about the origins of friendship reminds me of an exhibition I once saw called 'The Origins of Life'. Peering into the dark entrance of the Science Museum in London, I wondered if I was brave enough to go into the blackness and discover how the universe was made. Coming out the other end I was quite convinced that the universe began with a 'big bang' arising from fluctuations in a 'quantum vacuum'. I have since realized that it is not quite so straightforward as that! In the same way, we may wonder

The origin of friendship

whether friendships and the making of friends just 'happen' by chance like some 'big bang' theory. Or are there other explanations as to why we make friends? How do we account for the strength of feeling that many people have for their friends? What is it that causes people to feel this way about each other?

I would like to suggest four different but interlocking pieces to this puzzle of the source of friendship: its spiritual, social, psychological and sexual dimensions.

FRIENDSHIP AND SPIRITUALITY
We all want friends, because that is the way God has made us—to live in relationship with families, with human friends and with God himself.

The spiritual dimension to life has seen a resurgence in the last two decades of the twentieth century. Forests of trees have been felled in order to provide the pulp necessary for books on the New Age movement alone. With their combination of Eastern mysticism, occult practices, self-help psychology and idolizing of the god within, New Age writers are seeking to meet the needs of a spiritually starving world. For decades the Western world has been pursuing a materialistic dream, believing that there was a crock of gold at the end of the rainbow. But fruitless searches at the end of successive rainbows have left many people weary and disillusioned, with their inner emptiness still unsatisfied. A new search for meaning, purpose and value has begun, with a recognition that these are to be found in spiritual values.

The tragedy is that the Church and its message have by and large been rejected. This tragedy is of immense proportions because while New Age ideas focus on human dignity and potential, they fail to deal adequately with the failings of that same human nature. The damning evidence can be

Understanding friends

seen in our own lives. At times we are capable of producing tender acts of love, unfettered creativity and words that bring hope and healing. Yet in the same breath we can change like some Jekyll and Hyde character, revealing a selfish, grasping love of ourselves and destructive impulses, and producing thoughts and words of hate and malice. As one actor said of his profession: 'In our business everyone wants to be Jesus Christ, and ends up being Judas Iscariot.'

Diego Maradona, the Argentinian football player, shows clearly this glory and shame that is our humanness. The glory is seen in his

> . . . God-given talent that has produced such breathtaking performances on the field, when he could wriggle past one defender after another with the air of a man enjoying a leisurely stroll. Maradona was a legend who could hope to go down as the greatest sportsman of the decade.[1]

The shame is seen in his suspension from football through drug-taking, his involvement with prostitutes, and rumoured connections with the Mafia. A glittering career has come to a tarnished halt. The dilemma demonstrated in our own lives, and in Maradona's, is that when we see the glory and the shame of human nature we want one and not the other, but have to live with both.

Let's put this dignified and glorious aspect of human nature under the microscope and look more closely at what it is all about. The dignity that is within every human being is there because, as the Bible informs us, we are made in the image of God. Created human beings reflect their Creator. If you go into an art gallery and wander around you will be able to recognize certain paintings, even if you do not know what they are called, simply by the style of the artist. The

The origin of friendship

vibrant, almost crazed colours of Van Gogh or the stooping matchstick men of Lowry reveal the artists behind the art. They reflect something of the personality and character of the artist who took a virgin piece of canvas and made a masterpiece. All human beings bear within themselves the likeness of God, even though it has become grotesquely marred.

John Stott, the English preacher and author, has suggested a number of qualities that distinguish us as human beings. We are able to think and reason for ourselves; make moral choices; exhibit powers of artistic creativity; express our capacity for relationships of love; and explore our insatiable thirst for God.[2] These qualities reveal something of what God is like, and what he[3] wants to produce in us is that we should use these qualities to dignify our humanity. Let's focus on one of these qualities of humanness, the capacity for relationships of love. We have this capacity because God is love and an important consequence is that 'If God is love, then he is the ultimate source of all friendship.'[4] C.S. Lewis was right when, in writing about love, he described friendship as one of the distinctive expressions of this love.[5]

Because friendship has its origins in the way God has made us everyone wants friends, but the ultimate source of love and friendship is God himself. Although we may have many friends who enrich our life, until we meet God face to face and receive the friendship he offers, an insatiable thirst will remain.

FRIENDSHIP AND SOCIAL ORIGINS
The birth of a baby often results in various members of the wider family staking some kind of physiological claim. 'Hasn't he got his father's nose?', 'Her ears are just like

Understanding friends

Aunt Agatha's', 'Isn't his hair the same colour as his grandfather's?' This can reach the comical point where the poor parents wonder if they have contributed anything to their baby at all! In a genetic sense we do carry within us our parents and their parents and so on back through the generations. However, there is evidence to suggest that we also carry in us, in some unconscious way, the family or group in which we have been nurtured.

Dr Robin Skynner, one of the founders of both the Institute of Group Analysis and the Institute of Family Therapy, describes an exercise used to train family therapists. At the start of their training, before they can find out anything about each other, trainees are put in groups and asked to choose someone who reminds them of somebody in their family or who they feel would have filled a gap in their family. They are not allowed to speak. After finding a partner they talk about why they chose that partner. This process is repeated, the couple finding another couple and discussing why they chose that couple. The quartet then forms itself into a family, with each person taking on a different role. It transpires that when they talk about their family backgrounds and attitudes there are striking similarities. This 'Family Systems Exercise' shows that 'we're carrying around our families with us, somewhere inside us, and we're giving off signals which enable others with similar backgrounds to recognise us . . . . We signal, by our expression, postures and ways of moving, certain habitual emotional attitudes we have, which we share with other members of our family.'[6] Other psychologists talk about us taking our 'environment' (all that our family and upbringing both did and did not give us) with us wherever we go.

So our attraction to others and the development of friendship can be influenced by these signals which we give

The origin of friendship

out. The person we become friends with may appear to be very different from those within our family. If, for example, it is difficult in our family to express anger, it is often the case that the friends we choose, while different in many ways, may well have that same problem in expressing anger. Although we may be unaware of these factors, our family or lack of family may have a significant bearing on the origins of our friendships.

FRIENDSHIP AND PSYCHOLOGICAL NEED

Every human being who has ever existed has had needs. Lucy Irvine answered an advertisement for a 'Girl Friday' and spent a year with a man on a deserted island, without water or electricity. Far from being an idyllic paradise, it became a tropical nightmare. Lucy and George came to hate one another. They argued about everything, including sex, crude language, class differences, and intellectual abilities, but a time came when they were both so weak and ill that they gave up their differences because they needed each other. Lucy wrote: 'Our differences diminished as our mutual needs increased. We were companions in want.'[7] They recognized the truth of the famous words of the seventeenth-century poet, John Donne, 'No man is an island, entire of itself . . . any man's death diminishes me, because I am involved in Mankind.'[8] This need for others is part of us. The rock singer Sheena Easton voiced the views of many when she said that given a choice between living on a desert island alone and the prospect of dying, she would rather die.

A recent psychoanalytic textbook, *Our Need for Others and its Roots in Infancy*,[9] recognizes this basic need within human beings and suggests that the answer lies in the early months of life. Our need for others, be they family or

Understanding friends

friends, goes back to the day we were born and involves our deepest feelings. A baby is born dependent, both physically and psychologically: 'How mysterious a baby is, its personality still largely potential, and how helpless. Yet how powerfully it reaches out to us and touches the heart—for sustenance and for the relief of its distresses, but also for recognition.'[10]

In the early months of its life a baby sees people as objects. Over time these distant objects become people that the baby recognizes and can respond to. A relationship becomes established with its mother, father or some other person acting in this role. In this relationship there is communicated a whole range of feelings and emotions such as anger, love, hate, fear, pain, loss or joy. 'How can it manage such feelings, helpless as it is? It cannot—that is what the adult is for . . . it is the adult who mainly provides the context of its experiences.'[11] So when a baby experiences a pain in its stomach caused by gulping down its milk, all it can do is scream the place down. A baby has no concept of time and it makes no difference that it is 4.00 am and its parents have been asleep for only a few hours. It is the adult who must provide relief by taking away the pain, bringing the baby a sense of well-being. A baby then begins to gain the feeling and understanding that it is of some worth from those around it. A baby begins to develop its own sense of identity and separateness at a psychological level in what can be described as its 'inner world'. This inner world stays with us through adulthood and it is a vital part of our everyday lives.

Just as a baby grows in its sense of well-being by the response of the adults around, so now as adults we often grow in our sense of well-being by responding to those other adults who have become our friends. Our friends may be

The origin of friendship

able to help us regain a sense of well-being which we in turn can share in our friendships with others.

It is this strong psychological need for others that makes loneliness such a painful experience. The issues of friendship and loneliness are inextricably linked. While browsing through the index of a book called *Clergy Stress: The Hidden Conflicts in Ministry*,[12] I came across this entry: 'Friendship *see* Loneliness'. Loneliness has been described by Mother Teresa of Calcutta as the biggest problem of the twentieth century. Loneliness implies isolation and the lack of friends, the breakdown of relationships, no real communication, and our inner denial of our longing and need for others. Each of us has a psychological need for friends. The humanistic psychologist, Abraham Maslow, has produced a model of human development that he calls 'a hierarchy of human needs'. The first and most basic level is physiological—we need to be fed; the second is for safety and security—we need somewhere to live, with some kind of social structure; the third is to belong—most clearly seen in our ability to make friends. Maslow argues that it is only if we can reach this stage of belonging and making friends that we can progress as human beings. All else is merely survival. In case this sounds depressing, in chapter three we shall be looking at how to make friends.

FRIENDSHIP AND SEXUALITY

A semi-naked man walks out of the shower, and splashes on the latest body fragrance. As he walks through the hotel, women stop what they are doing to stare, until he meets a woman in the foyer. She reaches up to touch him and her hand caresses his body. 'Wear this cologne and women will take notice of you and want to caress you' is the message and it includes all the obvious sexual overtones which the

Understanding friends

mind imagines. We live in a world where sex is used to sell almost anything, with advertising reaching absurd levels. 'In a builders' merchant a poster hangs displaying a naked woman sitting astride a steel girder. She arches her back and thrusts out her breasts. The look on her face promises that if we hold up our ceilings with this beam then she will fulfil our wildest sexual dreams.'[13] When we talk of friendship and sexuality we need to step back from many of the current misinterpretations surrounding sex and sexuality.

One of the first statements the Bible makes about God is that he exists in relationship with 'others' (Genesis 1.26). God is not alone, and after his creation of Adam he declares, 'It is not good for man to be alone' (Genesis 1.18). Man alone would not be a true reflection of the likeness of God. The capacity to love requires someone to recognize that love. So God's answer is woman. Men and women, as distinct sexual beings, with the capacity for relationships of love with God, with each other, and with the world, reveal something of God's blueprint for every human being. When we long for relationship we are acting as God planned. We, like God, are looking for 'others' with whom to express this capacity for love. One word which sums up these ideas is 'sexuality'. But because it has become such an abused word, and because it frightens people even in this supposedly liberated society, it needs some definition.

There is a great deal of confusion about the subject of gender, sexual behaviour, and sexuality. It is important to clarify this if we are to see the role that sexuality plays in friendship. Every human is a sexual being, who is either male or female. The term 'gender' simply refers to whether we are male or female. The word 'sex' is used today as shorthand to mean 'sexual activity'. Sex, its promise of fulfilment and its ability to grab our attention in a purely instinctive, biological

The origin of friendship

way, is used relentlessly by advertisers in overt or subliminal ways, as we have already seen. It is a tragedy when something which God declares to be of fundamental importance and 'very good' (Genesis 1.27, 31) is prostituted and devalued. Sexuality can be defined as 'the capacity for intimate relationship', an idea that is profoundly biblical.

The creation narratives tell us that 'the making of man and woman as sexual beings is specifically linked with their creation in God's image.'[14] So what should we do with this sexuality, revealing as it does something of God's nature? We are to express it in relationships. 'Just as the Being of God himself is personal communion within the Trinity, so to be in the image of God is to be in personal communion with other persons.'[15] Adam needed Eve for reasons other than the production of children or the enjoyment of sexual activity. It was God's opinion that Adam's state of 'aloneness' (Genesis 2.18) was not a good thing. So within every human being our sexuality is a potentially creative drive which seeks out and finds security in relationships. 'Genesis 2 describes the human person at many levels of life: physical, emotional, relational, spiritual. Our sexuality covers all these . . . there is a sexual dimension to our affectionate relationships with men and women of the same and opposite sex, which needs to find appropriate and creative expression.'[16] Think for a moment of a mother and baby:

> This close contact between mother and child—mouth to breast, skin against skin, eye to eye—is the first sexual communication we make with another person. It is uncomplicated, natural and completely free from the sense that something dirty or nasty is happening. It expresses love and understanding and the need human beings have for one another, emotionally and spiritually, as well as physically.[17]

Understanding friends

Our second child, Toby, was born at home on our double bed. It had not been planned this way but one of the intense pleasures I had as a new father was being able to hold, feed, dress and care for my brand new son in a way I would have been denied had he been born in hospital. It was a tender, emotional and loving time which gave me a profound experience of the joy of being human, and which has enriched my understanding of sexuality. Some of the best expressions of our sexuality—the ability to bring pleasure to others, the fact that we can have feelings for others, and enjoyment of relationship—are seen in friendship.

One well-known friendship which illustrates these factors is the relationship between David and Jonathan (1 Samuel 17–20; 2 Samuel 1.2). Their friendship demonstrates an attraction to one another, an acceptance of their feelings for one another (their sexuality in the sense in which it has been explored here) and a recognition of God working in their lives.

Jonathan was the son of Israel's king, Saul, and he was heir to the throne. He did not have to work, never went hungry and had people to do whatever he commanded. Yet Jonathan was no sycophantic prince. When his father went to war Jonathan went with him and proved that he was a brave, skilled warrior who had put his trust in God; he was an ideal future king of Israel. However, that was not to be, since God had decided that the next king should be Jonathan's best friend, David. David, unlike Jonathan, did not have a privileged existence. The youngest of eight children, he was given fairly menial jobs to do like looking after the sheep in the family's agricultural business. David's first opportunity to prove God's confidence in him was a battle in which Saul and Jonathan were fighting. It was here that the renowned friendship between David and Jonathan began.

The origin of friendship

The enemy had a huge warrior, Goliath, who challenged all comers to single combat. In the whole of Israel no-one was willing to take up this challenge until David arrived on the scene. Out of a concern for God's honour, David said that he would fight Goliath. The king was so desperate that when he heard of David's willingness to fight he allowed him to go ahead, and we all know the end of the story. David killed Goliath and became a national hero. One of the witnesses was Jonathan.

Like all friendships, it began with having something in common. As a brave man himself, did Jonathan feel his heart stir when he saw David's courage? Whatever the cause, he saw something in David that drew him into a deep friendship. The Bible is quite explicit about this friendship: Jonathan 'became one in spirit with David, and he loved him as himself' (1 Samuel 18.1, see also 1 Samuel 20.17). Later, when Saul tried to kill David, Jonathan risked his life to warn him. A painful parting followed for these two close friends as 'they kissed each other and wept together—but David wept the most' (1 Samuel 20.42). They were never to meet again. David revealed his feelings for Jonathan when he heard of his death: 'I grieve for you, Jonathan my brother; you were very dear to me. Your love for me was wonderful, more wonderful than that of women' (2 Samuel 1.26). Michael, David's wife may not have been too happy to hear that, but it illustrates his true emotions for Jonathan. There is no suggestion that they had a homosexual relationship (forbidden in Leviticus 18.32 and 20.13), but they enjoyed expressing their God-given sexuality in feelings of affection and love for one another. This was the bedrock of a friendship which affirmed their mutual feelings, their faith in God and their struggles on behalf of the people of Israel. David and Jonathan's friendship reveals

Understanding friends

something of God in their ability to express attraction, love, commitment and giving to another.

We can see that the reason why we make friends with others has to do with spiritual, social, psychological and sexual causes. Not all elements will be prominent in all friendships but they will be there nonetheless, and it is important that we recognize their value and influence. These different dimensions to the source of friendships explain why friends are so important to us, but they do not in themselves guarantee friendship. In the next chapter we shall explore approaches to making friends.

3

Making friends

When I was a boy living in Glasgow, a family treat was to be taken to the circus at Kelvin Hall. Children rarely suspect the sadness behind the make-up smile of the clown or the cruelty involved in training wild animals to perform like pets, but they do sense the danger and drama of such acts as the high-wire tightrope walk. The performer climbs up and up and up, then, before a hushed audience and with the aid of a pole and a safety net, performs his death-defying feat of walking across the wire which spans the width of the big top. A child goes home from the circus with star-filled eyes, plenty to dream about and a sense of wonder and well-being at the excitement of it all.

The components of this circus act provide a helpful analogy with friendship. Friendships can be found at different levels, which can each help us negotiate life and bring to it that same sense of wonder and well-being. We need friendship at the most basic level as a safety net. It is part of the background which we sometimes feel we can do without, and most of the time don't even notice. Yet when it is needed, it is vital—it stops us falling flat on our faces and injuring ourselves. Claire Rayner, the well-known agony aunt, described how a friend helped by being that safety net for her and inadvertently started her off on her television career:

Understanding friends

We'd just moved to the suburbs and I didn't know a soul. After working for 12 years, I'd given up my nursing job at a London hospital before our first child, Amanda, was born. My husband, Des, was away at work all day and I was desperate to have a grown-up to talk to, I put a notice in a shop window. I think I can still remember the wording: 'Lonely little girl, 18 months, needs friend to play with. Her mother could use a friend too.' Somehow, an afternoon TV programme . . . heard about my advert. They asked me to come on the programme to talk about the anguish of a new mother stuck at home with a small baby.[1]

At another level we depend on friends to anchor, direct and help us, in the same way a tight-rope artist depends on a properly attached wire. We can rely on our friends not to let go of us when we need them. Yet it can sometimes surprise us who these friends are, and one of the most profoundly uplifting experiences in life is to discover the depths of friendship. Mike Yaconnelli tells the story of a teenage boy, who needed chemotherapy for cancer. A side-effect of the treatment is the loss of hair and sure enough all this boy's hair fell out. Baldness is a sensitive subject at any age, but for a teenager so conscious of what he looks like and what others think, it is traumatic. He was anxious about his return home. When the time came he was shown into a darkened room. When the lights were turned on he saw a banner that said 'Welcome Home' and his friends who had all shaved their heads so that he would not be the odd one out. Friends like this become part of the journey we travel as life unfolds. One of Britain's funniest comediennes, Dawn French (of French and Saunders), reflecting on a decade of acclaim and success, says; 'To be honest, the

Making friends

friendship I have with Jen is more important than the work—I'd rather be her friend till the day I die than keep the act till I die. And she feels the same way.'[2] What started out as a working relationship has developed into a friendship which has served as an anchor for the two women as difficult times have come and gone.

There are also some friendships which operate at more than one level. One day the telephone rang in our house and my wife, Judy, answered it. It was her friend, Heather. 'How are you?' she asked, no doubt expecting a conventional reply. When Heather told her that she was pregnant, Judy's screams of excitement could be heard all over the house. Judy wanted to know all the details (well, not quite all of them) as they chatted for what seemed like hours. Judy and Heather see each other for only a few hours at most, perhaps twice a year. Yet their friendship, forged during their schooldays thirty years ago, is still important to both of them. It is there, like a safety net to fall back into, a situation which has been brought about by distance. If we were ever to move back to the part of Lancashire where Heather lives, this friendship would assume a much greater significance. Friendships like this are crucial: they can help us find safety and rest when life becomes stormy. While there are some friends who anchor our lives at different points, we also need friends who can be carried along with us in the here-and-now, like the tight-rope walker's pole.

These are friends who help us balance our lives when things seem to be at their most precarious or when we feel that we are about to come crashing down. The pole is not just there for effect, it is needed for balance. This level of friendship requires an intimacy that men in particular find difficult. Writing about men, Roy McCloughry agrees that

Understanding friends

they are emotionally inarticulate and possess no personal language to describe their inner world. As a consequence,

> ... men's neglect of emotional expression causes great frustration in their relationships with woman and isolation from the possibility of intimacy with other men .... When it comes to friendship with other men there is a great deal of isolation and loneliness around. Men have colleagues and acquaintances, they may even have somebody with whom they have played squash every Friday night for the last 25 years, but they rarely have close and intimate friendships with other men .... There is an easy camaraderie among men who know that nothing intimate is going to be expected from them. But such a view of friendship is adequate only when life is kind. When crisis comes some men find that their friends fade away. But men who are prepared to take risks can find that appropriate self-disclosure deepens friendship with other men.[3]

All the men and women with whom I have discussed this subject have expressed a desire for this type of friendship, although some people are honest enough to admit their uncertainty about coping with such a depth of commitment.

An example from the life of Houdini, the famous escapologist, illustrates the kind of commitment required. He began his career as a tight-rope walker and one of the places where he performed was the Niagara Falls. He would walk along a tight-rope stretched across the Falls, hundreds of feet in the air, where a fall would be fatal. On one occasion he is reputed to have asked if anyone believed he could walk across pushing a wheelbarrow with a person sitting in it. The crowd had seen him do this so they said yes. Houdini turned to one member of the crowd and said 'Get in!'

Making friends

When it comes to friendships we acknowledge their importance in the lives of others but are reluctant to commit ourselves. While we believe that friendship is important and something which we want, we also harbour a nagging feeling that somehow this sort of friendship is for others, and not for us. It may be that we are recovering from a broken friendship and are unsure about committing ourselves again, or have never had a friendship requiring this level of commitment. We may find it difficult to express our inner feelings. The people in the crowd were happy to watch Houdini walk the tight-rope, but it was quite another matter to do it themselves. So it is now time to discuss, step by step, how we can form and develop friendships.

In my childhood, because of the frequent moves to various parts of the country which were associated with my father's job, I often had to leave friends behind. I became accustomed to the slow and sometimes painful business of starting from scratch and making new friends. I found that in the process of building friendships, we generally go through four stages.

MEETING PEOPLE
It is impossible to make friends without meeting people, something which is much more difficult in our British culture than in many others. Once, while travelling through Spain, I sat next to two ladies on the train. One of them turned to me and said 'Do you want a cookie?' I will leave you to guess where they came from—the important thing is that a conversation began which could have led to a friendship. The idea of such an event happening in Britain is made almost unthinkable by the 'great British reserve'. Anyone who talks to other passengers is considered distinctly odd. The degree of openness in some other cultures

Understanding friends

makes it easier for people to discover the common ground which is vital to the start of a friendship.

One of the advantages of being Christians is that if we move to a new area and join a new church, we find a ready-made family and source of potential friends. Recently, while enjoying a meal at a wedding reception, I talked to one of the bridesmaids, a shy person who had just moved to another part of the country, about how she went about making friends. She said that although she was friendly with the other teachers in her school, none of them lived locally, so she had to make friends elsewhere. She went to the local branch of the Young Rotarians (a social group of business people who organize charitable events) and volunteered to take part in their soup run for the homeless. By simply doing something with other people of her age, she soon found others with whom she had common interests. Yet she remembered how hard it was to walk into a room full of strangers and sit on her own, and this is something that most people find it very difficult to do.

BUILDING A FRIENDSHIP
The next stage is to take a number of steps with the deliberate intention of building a friendship. Once we have met people, there are various ways in which we can make it easier for ourselves to form friendships.

We can begin by trying to *think positively*. Each encounter is a learning experience, not some ordeal that we force ourselves to go through, like going to the dentist. Friendship does not begin easily if we have to grit our teeth to get through the experience. Yet for many people this is how the real business of making friends starts. This may mean that we have to do some work on how we view ourselves. If we think 'nobody will want me as a friend', it can become a self-

Making friends

fulfilling prophecy. Your image of yourself is important and it is a subject we shall look at in more detail in a later chapter.

We can, after all, *create opportunities* for other people to talk to us. Make it easy for them to start a conversation, even if it is initially about the weather. Ruth was an attractive but shy young woman, who until recently often felt depressed. This showed on her face and she found that complete strangers would say to her, 'Cheer up, it may never happen.' I can still remember how difficult it was, when I first met Ruth, to have a conversation with her. She would answer all my questions with a straight 'yes' or 'no' and make no further comment or effort to continue the conversation. This meant that any attempt to sustain a conversation was like an inquisition. It was a great encouragement when Ruth began to take the risk of forming new relationships and started to change in many ways. She now quite freely talks to others and makes friends.

Next, it is important that we are aware of the *unspoken 'rules' that govern social situations*. If in our first conversation with someone we tell them everything about ourselves they may feel overwhelmed, and distance themselves from us. I learned this when, after an enjoyable evening with a girl at a party, I asked her to go out the next day. When I went to meet her she told me that she didn't want to go out after all. That was that, or so I thought. A couple of weeks later I learned from a friend that the girl had said she still wanted to go out with me—which left me confused. Being fairly new to the boy–girl relationship business, I was still learning that relationships take time. The girl was interested in me but wanted to move at a pace she could handle. We never did go out.

It helps not to *judge by appearances*. The stereotyped views we have of ourselves and of others can greatly hinder

Understanding friends

initial conversations. In the film *Shirley Valentine*, a downtrodden middle-aged housewife escapes from her dreary existence by going on holiday to Greece and then decides to stay there. As she thinks about her past she dwells on her rebellious schooldays and her jealousy of another schoolgirl, 'goody-goody' Marjorie Majors. Twenty-five years later they bump into one another as Marjorie gets out of a Rolls Royce, and she invites Shirley to her penthouse flat. Shirley is shocked to discover that Marjorie is a call-girl. They talk about their time at school:

MARJORIE: Did you realize that I wanted to be like you?
SHIRLEY: And I wanted to be like you. If only we had known we could have been great mates, close. You're off to Paris now.
MARJORIE: But I'd rather be here talking to you.

On their parting Marjorie gives Shirley a hug and a kiss and Shirley thinks to herself, 'There was real affection in that kiss, the sweetest I'd known in years.'[4] Shirley and Marjorie had judged by appearances and as a result missed out on what for them both could have been an important and close friendship.

Another point to bear in mind is to try to *give clear signals*. When we want to talk to someone, it helps to establish eye contact and respond to their conversation with smiles or nods. These examples of non-verbal communication are so common we may not realize that we are doing it, in either a positive or a negative way. While working in a psychiatric hospital, I discovered how accurately patients, despite their mental health problems, were able to discern whether a member of staff thought of them as real human beings or as just a job to be done.

There is no substitute for *taking risks*. It may be easier to say 'reveal yourself' than to do it, but this is a vital step that

Making friends

we all need take. Show that you want to be noticed, not by outlandish behaviour, such as that to which adolescents are prone, but by simply saying 'Hello, it's nice to meet you.' If the person does not respond or just smiles and goes away, don't take this as a fatal snub, thinking that there will be no other chances to meet people. Part of the risk-taking is giving other people choices. Any relationship is two-way, so if we have begun a conversation, we should allow the other person room to respond. If we have enjoyed the other person's company, then we should tell them so. It is a risk but one that often begins a friendship.

We need to *respect other people's boundaries*. If, for example, we have discovered something about the other person and they have taken a risk in telling us, then it may not be a good idea to probe or try to tease out all the facts. Someone I played squash with told me over lunch afterwards that his marriage was going through some difficulties. The next time we met, I did not ask about his marriage in particular, but I did ask how he was feeling, thus giving him the opportunity to talk if he wished. Allowing this acquaintance to begin to share his feelings and emotions has established a warm, close friendship. Yet my friend had to make the approach he was comfortable with in order to bring this about.

These different steps will not guarantee friendship, any more than reading a book on cars will make you a mechanic or reading a recipe book will make you a chef. But they might help you make progress in some of those relationships which otherwise become stuck in the very early stages.

KEEPING UP A FRIENDSHIP
Having taken steps to build a friendship, we need to reach the next stage in discovering some common ground that

Understanding friends

can sustain and nurture a newly-formed friendship. This was the problem of a girl called Sue. She was six inches taller than most of the girls her age and taller than many of the boys as well. She felt a gnawing anxiety as she started her new school. Would the new girls accept her and treat her as normal? As she assembled with hundreds of others in the school hall she glanced across the sea of heads to find herself staring at another girl, the same age and the same height. They became inseparable friends. Similarly, during our initial encounters in meeting and talking with people, we look for common ground around which a tentative friendship can be formed.

A health visitor in my church established a group called 'Baby and Co' for mothers with new babies, many of them first-time mothers. A few were friends already, but for many of them the group became a place to meet others undergoing similar experiences and to form friendships. Each person had the opportunity to talk and listen. There was room for them to begin to share their fears and frustrations about such matters as their baby not sleeping, their interfering mother-in-law, their sense of loss at no longer going to work, and at times their guilt at feeling angry with their little bundle of noise. It was a huge relief to discover that others, whom they had perceived to be perfect mums, felt just as frustrated. Having been able to talk about their babies, many people were then free to talk about themselves and to share ideas, hopes, emotions, and fears. As a result several lasting friendships were formed. Friendship needs this common ground to allow us to take the initial steps without the fear of falling flat on our faces.

We have seen how friendship requires us to listen. Now that we've begun to observe the process involved in making friends, we move on to two key factors which come into

Making friends

play at this listening stage. They are simple, obvious and often neglected. One is simply being able to listen. This was Helen's conclusion when she went to her doctor suffering from depression:

> He saw me first of all, and I realize now, looking back, that he was a very depressed person himself. I remember him . . . saying 'Life is a very lonely business.' He just talked about how he felt about his own life. It seems to be a very common thing when you're in a deep depression, people come and tell you how much a struggle their life is. It's very, very few people who listen.[5]

After finishing at university and before going to theological college to become a Baptist minister, I spent a year at home working for British Rail. The Baptist church I was attending was without a minister, so when the father of one of my mother's friends died, I was asked to go and see the widow. Visiting someone who had been bereaved was a new experience for me. So with fear, trepidation and much prayer I called round at her home. I was shown into the lounge and the daughter went to make me a cup of tea. Fumbling for words, I said something like 'I am sorry to hear about your sad news, can you tell me a bit about your husband?' That was all I did. It seemed a bit artificial to trot out the Bible verses that talk of the 'sting' of death being removed, so in my ignorance I simply sat and listened. Before I left, feeling that I had been of very little use, I prayed with the lady. I now realize that I had done the most helpful thing possible and that was to listen. That lady told many other people what a help my visit had been. I listened because I did not know what else to do, but listening is a vital skill, and it can be acquired. There are skills we can learn that will enhance friendship.

Understanding friends

Learning to listen means learning to hear. The physical ability to hear is a very important one which, sadly, many people lose as they get older. This loss makes communication much more difficult, especially when the sufferer denies it and wonders why everybody is mumbling all the time! The ability to listen at a psychological level and actually take in what the other person is saying is every bit as vital as our physical ability to hear. Listening is important. Dr Paul Tournier has written:

> It is impossible to over-emphasize the immense needs human beings have to be listened to . . . in most conversations, although there is a good deal of talk, there is not real listening; such conversations are no more than a dialogue of the deaf.[6]

It is difficult to listen if we are preoccupied with ourselves. If we constantly think about ourselves we become deaf to other people. Mandy and Jill were two best friends who left home to share a flat. For the first six months all was well until Jill was made redundant. They managed to struggle through financially, but when Mandy called round to see me she was at breaking point. In an angry outburst Mandy said, 'I've had enough of her constantly telling me life's tough, life's not fair. She says, "It's okay for you, at least you have a job." But what about me?' Mandy demanded, 'I'm a person, I've got needs as well.' Mandy and Jill's friendship had reached crisis point because Jill was not listening.

Unfortunately we often don't realize when we are so wrapped up in ourselves that we are not really listening to what people are saying. Inevitably if we are suffering bereavement, redundancy or some other major crisis, there will be a natural self-protective mechanism operating, so

Making friends

that for a short time we concentrate solely on the business of survival. This naturally makes it more difficult to hear what others are saying but most people understand. It becomes a problem when it is part of our continuing way of relating to others.

Sarah called round at the house, just to say 'Hello', but the smudged mascara round her eyes told me that she had been crying. We sat down and she poured out her anger and pain that she never had friends and that no-one was interested in her. She hated work, she hated church and she wished she could move away and make a new start somewhere else where people were more friendly. In the past I had noticed that Sarah always talked about herself but showed very little interest in others. When the spotlight was on her she was the life and soul of the party, but when it was not, she withdrew into the shadows, almost sulking and waiting for someone to notice her little girl 'no-one is talking to me' act. We started talking about the 'real' Sarah, and a picture came to light of a vulnerable, frightened little girl who felt that unless she talked about herself, she would become totally insignificant. Over a period of time we explored how her view of herself was expressed in the way she acted and responded to those around her. Sarah began to see that her preoccupation with herself was actually pushing away the offers of friendship which others were making to her. By thinking about how others felt she began to realize that the spotlight isolates one person from the rest, and she discovered that when it was off her there were plenty of other people standing around in the shadows with her.

Listening requires us to put ourselves on one side and start thinking and responding to the other person as another person, rather than as a mirror of ourselves. It is only

Understanding friends

then that we really listen. Anne Long describes listening like this:

> If you listen to me I feel valued, you give me your time, acceptance—something I may never have had—and a relationship with another human being—something I may have problems with. You share the burden of my grief, my loneliness, my frustration, my indecision, my guilt. I've been alone with it so far. You let me think my thoughts aloud and sometimes, that way, I find answers—or at least discover where to look for them.[7]

Not all friendships can offer this quality of listening and provide such a level of insight into ourselves but there is the potential in every friendship for people to be valued and approved of. How does real listening take place? Often in the early stages of a friendship, we test it in order to assess the type of relationship it might become.

We want to find out if the other person can be relied on. We have all kinds of unspoken questions which we want answered before we commit ourselves in friendship? 'Is he going to tell others about me?', 'How will she respond when I tell her something she may not approve of?', 'Will I be treated as a problem to be solved?', 'Will he lose interest after a few weeks?' Often in the early stages of a friendship, we look for confirmation that this person really is a friend. 'Does she ring me up or say she wants to meet me again or is it always me doing the hard work? Is it always me who makes the first move?' If so, the friendship founders and we are back to square one. This is all part of the listening test to which we subject people at a totally unconscious level. It is so much part of us we are not even aware that we are doing it.

Making friends

There is also a detective test that potential friends are subjected to. They have to find out information about each other for themselves. Sherlock Holmes never fails to amaze me. With the smallest snippets of information he is able to piece together clues and track down the culprit. Like Dr Watson, his much put-upon sidekick, I am always two steps behind. Few of us are expert detectives like the fictional Holmes, Morse, Miss Marple, Poirot, Colombo, Wexford or Dalgleish, but as we move towards friendship with someone, we can all pick up clues which they have scattered around during the course of our relationship so far. The situation works both ways, of course, with us leaving clues for them. These clues may be discovered in a person's way of dressing, tone of voice, behaviour, and what is called 'body language'. These clues, if we pick them up, can be extremely useful because they reveal how a person really feels.

Dave rang up to see if he could come round to my house and talk about an important decision he had to make. Dave had been one of the young people in my previous church only fifteen miles away from where I was now working. When he arrived to see me, we had a pleasant conversation, but not one which in my estimation justified his fifteen-mile drive. Several months later when I saw him again he told me his view of our conversation. Three weeks before I had seen him, my wife had given birth to our son, Toby. Naturally my wife and I were delighted—but the lack of sleep caused by our new son had obviously taken a greater toll on me than I had imagined. David told me that when he came to see me I looked awful, as though I needed matchsticks to prop my eyes open. I could hardly string a coherent sentence together. Consequently he decided that my need was greater than his and he decided not to bother me with the real issue which he wanted to talk about. My

Understanding friends

perception of myself was that I was a little tired but still able to talk to people. David's perception, based on the clues my body was sending out, was a more accurate picture of how I was. An important part of friendship is noticing the clues our friends leave, consciously or unconsciously, and coming to the right conclusions.

There is also a comprehension test that we expect friends to pass. In our conversations and in our listening, people need to know not only that we have heard what they have said but that we have also understood. When I was at school one of the weekly classes was English comprehension. This was the subject which many of us hated most, mainly because of the teacher, Mrs Jones. She was strict and demanding, with a look which froze us to our seats, and a tongue like a rapier. She would give us a passage from a novel and then expect us to answer questions on it. We all sat praying that we would not be asked a question, breathing a sigh of relief when her gaze swept past, and sinking into despair when she looked one of us in the eye and asked what he or she understood about the passage. It wasn't enough to show that we had read the passage; Mrs Jones was trying to get us to understand, to question, and to interact with the texts we were reading.

Friends want to know whether we have understood them. When we are listening to other people we need some understanding not only of what they say but also of what they mean. If one friend tells me she is feeling a little bit under the weather, I take that quite seriously because she is one of those people who go on and on without complaining; what she means is that things are really pretty awful. Another friend may say the same thing, but it does not concern me to the same extent because he complains more readily. Sometimes our listening prompts us to ask questions

Making friends

not because we are nosey, but out of a desire to understand the person with whom we are building a friendship.

Listening, then, is vital to the healthy development of friendship. It requires an awareness that we need to learn to put our needs to one side and focus on what the other person says by his or her words and actions. It also demands the acknowledgement of what we feel at an intuitive level and a desire to understand the other person. If we possess these characteristics then we are a long way down the road of being a friend to others and discovering the friendship which they can give to us, but there is still one more stage in the development of a friendship.

COMMITMENT

Friendships need to pass through a further stage of risking and trusting. I have always wanted to parachute out of an aeroplane and experience the thrill of hurtling towards the ground at hundreds of miles an hour and then, with one pull of a ripcord, be able to float gently down to the ground. This remains an unfulfilled ambition. Yet part of me wonders whether I really could do it. For those brief seconds outside the aeroplane I would have to trust the parachute and that does entail some risk. An instructor may tell you that statistically parachuting is safer than crossing the road, but it does not seem that way.

Entering into a friendship at any level requires a degree of trust and we will discuss why some people find this particularly difficult in the next chapter. Trust is a necessary part of any relationship. No matter how we met our friend, how many common interests we have, or how skilled our listening has become, a point comes where we need to commit ourselves to sharing something of the real 'you' or 'me' with the other person.

Understanding friends

The real person in each of us is often very different from the person whom others see in us. Many psychotherapists, psychiatrists, psychologists and counsellors talk about the 'child' within each of us. Why have they used this image of a child? What is it about childhood which communicates so much? As I look at my children I am struck by a number of things that are vitally important for our adult lives.

There is the vulnerability of a child. Children are fragile, both physically and psychologically. For a baby to grow into a healthy child, he needs careful nurturing. He needs to be fed, changed, cuddled and loved. One psychiatrist, who is considered by his patients to be very caring, has spent many years in analysis coming to terms with the fact that he himself has been unable to form friendships other than at a surface level. When he starts talking about the 'child' in him all he sees is despair:

> Of course it goes back to childhood .... Do you know the Hans Anderson story, is it The Snow Queen? You know, the boy has a splinter of ice in his heart. It's like that ... they [the splinters] got stuck there and made things seem distorted, so that the person saw only the bad side of things. Some fragments even got into the hearts of a few people and then something terrible happened—these hearts turned into blocks of ice.[8]

Jesus had stern words to say about those who harmed vulnerable children and the consequences of destroying their ability to trust (Matthew 19.6).

Then there is the dependence of a child. Children need parents, people who will help them get dressed, make them food, take them to school, laugh at their corny jokes (often the same ones that parents told when they were the same age), help them to read, put plasters on their grazed knees,

Making friends

dry them when they come out the bath, and put them to bed. This mirrors our ultimate need for God; but as we saw in chapter two, a child needs another person to be there for her in order that she can grow properly into adulthood and fulfil her God-given potential.

There is a child's ability to believe and trust. Each night I tell my daughter a story I have made up. The current series of stories is about Martin the Martian and her favourite part is when I speak Martian. She asked me one night where I had learnt Martian and I told her quite straight-faced that I learnt it at university. She said, 'I thought so, because you speak it very well.' At some stage I will have to confess—but at the moment she trusts what her daddy says. Jesus talked about a child's ability to trust when he called children to him and spent time with them. He used them to teach adults about trusting God (Matthew 18.2–5; 19.13–15; Luke 18.15–17). Trust is a vital basis of any relationship.

Another characteristic of a child is creativity. Theirs is an exciting world of make-believe, adventure and discovery. Questions like 'What does Jesus wear when he goes to bed at night?' may be amusing to adults but also demonstrate a common-sense approach to life. The question 'Why?' is asked again and again. The walls of a child's bedroom are covered with artistic masterpieces which could teach Picasso a thing or two. Life is there to be lived and enjoyed in as creative a way as possible.

Finally most children have the ability to make friends. They seem to do it so naturally and easily by just being themselves. At the seaside on holiday, at the park, in their road—you name the place and most children can make friends there. Some of these friendships are transitory but the ability which they demonstrate is to be valued.

Understanding friends

Similarly in adulthood the 'child' within us is vulnerable, dependent, wants to believe and trust, is creative and needs a friend. However, as we become adults we learn that there are times when we need to protect ourselves. The adult world we live in can be a hostile, threatening place. As we make friends we rediscover what children already know—that part of friendship is showing other people what we are really like. We can then arrive at the point of risking and trusting. If any relationship is to progress beyond superficial friendship, this stage cannot be avoided. The fact that there are those around with whom we can be seen at our worst and still feel accepted and valued, that there are other human beings to whom we matter, makes life seem worth living. I am reminded of Helen, who described herself in this bleak way: 'I won't marry . . . I can't form relationships—I couldn't form a relationship with a dog or a cat . . . I'm hopeless at it . . . I have no conception of my sexuality'; yet she went on to say of her therapist, 'I trust her, which I don't think I can say about any other human being in my life.'[9]

We don't want another person's sympathy or good advice—we want them to feel, in part, what we feel. In all deep friendships, an empathy takes place. Empathy means an ability to enter into what another person feels. When we are on the receiving end of empathy, we feel that we are not alone, that there is somebody with us who understands, who feels, who is moved by what moves us. Remember the biblical injunction to 'Rejoice with those who rejoice and mourn with those who mourn' (Romans 12.15). That is empathy and it is a practical expression of love.

Part of risking and trusting is overcoming the fear of other people's response when we tell them something which they may not like. We want friends to like us, no matter what we do.

Making friends

We need friends to listen and to understand, we need to be able to take risks and trust in them, and they in turn need those qualities in us. We become like a pair of mirrors reflecting images backwards and forwards, revealing how we see and are seen by one another. That is both the privilege and responsibility of friendship which in turn is both exciting and frightening. It is our Christian friends who are often the best help in our growth as Christians. They can see our potential as a disciple and as friends they can highlight those areas that cause problems.[10] However our fears can prevent us from looking at ourselves in the mirror of another person's friendship. The reasons for this may be revealed when we make friends with our past.

4

Making friends with ourselves

The sun beat down as I lay on the beach, enjoying the refreshing breeze as it gently cooled my skin. No worries, no work, no demands, no telephone to answer, no deadline to meet. Nothing disturbed this tranquil scene, until I heard a familiar ringing sound in my ear. All too quickly the dream faded and another day had dawned. Not surprisingly, with dreams like that, I am conscious of a part of me which would like to be a millionaire. When I saw a newspaper headline that ran 'Millionaire: the secret of his success' I wanted to read more. The millionaire's philosophy was quite simple: 'I'm good at making friends. My motto is simple: one more friend, one more opportunity.' I thought to myself, 'If that's what it takes to be a millionaire then perhaps I don't want to be one after all. All he is doing is rationalizing his using of his so-called "friends". Pounds and profit obviously matter more than people.' I was surprised at the strength of my reaction to this comment which came close to anger. I have learnt that when I get angry it is always about something that is important to me. As I reflected on this I discovered that I was thinking about the people who had used me in the past, the people I once considered friends but who had let me down.

It seems that the past always has the ability to haunt the present. A song by the American folk singer Tracy Chapman puts it this way:

Making friends with ourselves

Our own ancestors
Are hungry ghosts
Closets so full of bones
They won't close

But all my ghosts they find me
Like my past they think they own me
In dreams and dark corners they surround me
Till I cry.[1]

These skeletons in cupboards from our past to which Tracy Chapman refers need examination because they can hinder our ability to make friends here and now. We need to learn how we can make friends with our past. One thing that all these skeletons have in common is that they have affected the way we view ourselves—our self-image or our sense of self.

When I was a boy I was involved in a gymnastic display, where we built a human pyramid. We were fine at first, but as the weight increased and our muscles grew tired, the base of the pyramid began to wobble. Seconds later the whole pyramid collapsed and catapulted the smallest boy, on top of the pyramid, into the air. Relationships need a firm foundation—a sense of self-worth—and if the foundation is insecure then, like the pyramid on its wobbly base, the whole relationship begins to collapse. We need a secure base from which we can reach out to others; they in turn can help us see the foundations of our friendship in a new light, realizing that these may also at times need attention.

We need to accept ourselves because we are important, a fact recognized by the apostle Paul. He identified some of the skeletons in his closet and wrestled with their impact on his life.[2] While he described himself as the world's

Understanding friends

worst sinner, he also enjoyed life because Christ lived in him.[3] He could clearly see the dangers of his past but he was content to accept his life as a servant of Christ, no matter how much difficulty that gave rise to.[4] The result was a person whose character is a marvellous balance of patience and impatience, toughness and tenderness, anger and affection, prayer and action. Here was a real person who had real friends (Romans 16). To use contemporary terms, Paul's 'self concept' (what he knew about himself) and Paul's self-esteem (what he felt about himself) combined to give a healthy self-image. He had a secure base, while being mindful of some of its imperfections. What we think about ourselves impinges on what we feel about ourselves, which in turn affects how we relate and respond to other people, especially friends. Our skeletons are very important. King David is an example of someone who needed to come to terms with his past. The skeleton of his adultery with Bathsheba (2 Samuel 11–12) returned to haunt him and had an influence on his family, the people of Israel and the way he worshipped (see Psalm 51). Who knows, if Jonathan had lived, as David's closest friend he may have helped prevent David's disastrous affair with Bathsheba.

In order to deal with our skeletons we shall explore how to live with our past and how to live in the present. The Book of Proverbs tells us: 'A man's spirit sustains him in sickness but a crushed spirit who can bear?' (18.14). There are many ways in which a person's spirit can be crushed, always with devastating consequences for their self-image. There are four main areas from our past that can have a vital influence on the development of our self-image; they are our psychological development, our family life, our schooling, and any traumatic events that may have befallen

Making friends with ourselves

us. Each of them plays an important part in the way we form a secure base and a healthy self-image.

WHAT MAKES US TICK?
The human body and the human mind are both immensely complicated. 'What makes us tick?' is a question with no easy answer. Yet a consensus of knowledge exists, based on psychological theories and clinical observation, which points us in a certain direction. The psychologist Dorothy Rowe describes in simple terms some of our psychological development which has great bearing on how we make or fail to make friends.

> When we were babies we had a set of beliefs which joined us to everything. Everything we encountered was interesting. Every person we met was a friend. We were our own best friend. Then we started to find that there were parts of our environment which were dangerous to explore. We found that sometimes our most wonderful mother disappeared and a most dangerous person came in her place. When we worked out that this most dangerous person was actually our mother being angry or unhelpful, we were confused about when it was safe to be close to her and when not. We found, too, that sometimes we were not our own best friend, because we would get ourselves into trouble. So, gradually, we collected quite a number of conclusions which served to cut ourselves off from other people, our environment, our past and our future, and from ourselves. Thus we discovered one of the great dilemmas of life.[5]

The dilemma is that there is part of us that wants to reach out in relationship to others because that is the way God made us, and yet, living apart from him, we will

Understanding friends

always be looking for the perfect relationship or the perfect friend. The Book of Genesis accounts not only for this desire in us to seek others, but also for the consequences when we do reach out to them. Earliest man and woman discovered that, paradoxically, in trying to be like God they began to damage the image of God they themselves carried. Conflict, an unwillingness to take responsibility for their actions, deceit, shame, fear and vulnerability became part of every person's humanness. Men and women discovered that relationship brought great joy and great sadness. Their vulnerability demanded defences to keep people at a distance, to prevent them getting close enough to cause further pain. Babies, children and adults learn this again and again.

Irene had very few close friends, though many acquaintances. She talked to me about her loneliness, caused, she felt, by an incident in her past. As a young mother she was very happy with a new baby boy when she was told the devastating news that she had a brain tumour. Thankfully, most of the growth was removed but the doctors could not guarantee her that it would not grow again. As a consequence she held back from getting too emotionally involved with her son and her husband. Her reasoning was that if she were to die it would be easier for her son, husband and friends to cope. Her lack of emotional involvement was not a lack of love; it was her way of defending others from what she thought would be immense pain. The cost that Irene paid was that she was never to become a real friend to her son and increasingly she found that she kept herself apart from other people as well.

We are left then wanting friends but are sometimes fearful of the process required to make friends. Our experience of being ourselves, or of 'me' being 'me', can be an import-

Making friends with ourselves

ant positive or negative influence on our ability to initiate and sustain friendship with others.

FAMILY BACKGROUND

Our early life as part of a family can have a significant effect on us. When Amy came home with her exam results, she was naturally excited, and thought her mother would be pleased with her 6 'A' grades and one 'B'. Rushing into the house she triumphantly handed the piece of paper over to her mother with a beaming grin. Her mother took the paper, read it and said in a cool, matter of fact voice 'You didn't get an "A" for French.' Amy's grin became a grimace. Her excitement at doing something really well was replaced by a sense of despair. 'What do I need to do to get her to love me?' Amy asked herself. This pattern of rejection and never being able to please her mother had several consequences for Amy.

One was that she viewed herself as worthless and unwanted. In fact she had been the result of an unwanted pregnancy and her mother's anger at this child robbing her of the life she wanted was made clear to Amy again and again. Not surprisingly, Amy developed depression as an adult, yet could not explain why she was depressed until we began to explore her past. Amy also found it difficult to maintain friendships. Her need for someone who would really like and approve of her made it difficult for her to accept any criticism, even from a friend. It made her feel that nobody wanted her, an echo from the past. Knowing that her mother did not want her made Amy extremely sensitive to rejection.

Jenny Firth-Cozens, a psychologist at Leeds University, has done some research on critical parents. She surveyed 170 young doctors and discovered that the greatest cause of

Understanding friends

stress was not long working hours or lack of sleep but the echoes of past relationships with parents. Dr Firth-Cozens concluded:

> The effect of early family experiences on a person's life is often dismissed as a cliché. But past relationships can be the underlying cause of stress at work and of conflict with authority figures . . . . We have to recognise that the way we treat children does affect their lives as adults. Even so, with therapy, it is possible to change the way we see ourselves and reduce the destructive aspects of self-criticism. It is possible to separate the baggage of childhood from what is happening . . . now.[6]

It can be added that the value of friendship is such that it too can be just as helpful and healing as therapy for many people. The trouble is that the past does hinder the development of close friendships.

Most people deal with rejection and hurt in the past in one of two ways. We tell ourselves that we will not be hurt in this way again and build up our defences. But we can then become so heavily defended from what we perceive to be attack from outside, that we pull up the drawbridge and stay trapped in the castle of our lives. As the siege goes on we can reach the desperate point of starvation as we run out of food and water. Psychologically, people are starving for lack of love, affection and friendship. Another way of trying to deal with rejection is to develop friendships at a superficial level. On the surface we appear fine, but when we are alone we are painfully aware of our deep unhappiness. Kriss Akabussi, a British medal-winning athlete always seems to be wearing a huge grin. His joy at winning a race is evident for millions to see on their television screens. But behind his huge grin Kris Akabussi has a very different story to tell.

Making friends with ourselves

He has described the effect on him of having been fostered from the age of five:

> We moved so many times my memory is of being torn away from people I had become fond of and I learned never to let myself feel secure or that this was really home. I didn't even have a favourite toy to take with me. I coped as children do, but I can see now that it's had a lasting effect. Everyone thinks I am outgoing and make friends easily, but the truth is I don't let anyone really close to me. I have very few intimate friends and even with my wife, whom I love and value very much, I hold something back. I learned very young that trusting people led to pain.[7]

The lack of a family has had a profound effect on Akabussi and on countless others. They live with the knowledge that no-one ever loved them enough to stay around. The very friendships that they need, they often cannot make. Yet Kriss Akabussi is coming to terms with this loss in his past. He has become a Christian and says:

> ... it has given new meaning to my life. One of the reasons, people have suggested, is that Christianity is a way of getting a father at last, the father figure I never had. The Father in Heaven is everything I wanted my father to be.... And knowing what a wonderful thing it is to be a father, trying to get it right for my kids.[8]

Kriss Akabussi is learning to make friends with his past, even if he still has feelings and memories which hurt.

It is not only critical or absent parents who can hinder our ability to see ourselves in a healthy light. Another source of tension within the life of our family is how we get on, or don't get on, with our brothers or sisters. Just imagine for a moment

Understanding friends

how traumatic it is to discover that you are no longer the centre of your parents' world. 'Mummy said she was going to hospital but why did she have to come back with "that". It's noisy and smelly and everyone goes mad over it, taking pictures, and they won't let me in. I get stuck with Granny and she can't even cook properly. What's more she's never heard of McDonald's or Postman Pat spaghetti. Daddy says aren't we lucky to have such a special little girl, but what about me? Don't I count? Aren't I your special little boy any more? That baby's sitting on Mummy's lap again, why can't I. It's not fair, Mummy has told me that I'm a big boy and I don't need to sit on her lap anymore. Even when I hold the baby they shout at me. It's not my fault I nearly dropped her.'

This imaginary monologue could go on and on, and demonstrates how a child can feel resentment, guilt and confusion about the new arrival who has become his rival. If a brother felt insecure beforehand, the new baby can become a ready-made explanation as to why he does not feel sufficiently loved. As a consequence older brothers or sisters often do the most awful things to their siblings, such as taking the brakes off the buggy and pushing it down a hill, nudging them down the stairs, putting them in the toilet, cutting off their hair and so on. These are just some of the ways in which children have reacted to their sense of hurt, loss or changed identity. Susie Orbach comments:

> Sibling rivalry is a pervasive phenomenon that can dog a person through adult life, not only affecting their relationships with their brothers and sisters, but influencing how they respond to colleagues and friends and their own children.[9]

The sense of not being what our parents really wanted because they went and got another one, yet not having any

Making friends with ourselves

real proof of this, leaves many adults with ambiguous feelings. Questions arise for older siblings such as, 'Do they really want me as a friend? Why do I feel I have to compete all the time?', and, most devastating of all, 'They really wanted a girl and all they got was me, a boy.' Younger siblings, especially the 'baby' of the family, ask other questions, 'Why can't I get my own way? Won't they let me be me? I'm not a baby any more.' Siblings can become stuck with family stereotypes which they spend much of their adult life trying to escape. One of the casualties is often friendship.

Acknowledging that we feel this way about our brothers or sisters can allow us to outgrow stereotypes and discover the ability to forgive past injustices.

LIFE AT SCHOOL
Much of our childhood is spent at school. While some people think this was the best time of their life, for others it was the worst. The school playground may look harmless enough—a grey concrete apron where children are busy skipping, kicking tennis balls about and rushing around in pursuit of their imaginary games. On the surface playtime looks like children having fun, using up their apparently boundless energy. On closer inspection, the playground is more like a battlefield, where children fight for control of their friends. The casualties of this particular war are those same friends. There are the familiar refrains: 'If you don't do what I say I won't be your friend', 'You can't come to my birthday party unless you give me the answers', 'If you tell the teacher, I won't like you any more.'

A recent study has shown that 50 per cent of schoolchildren are bullied, yet rarely tell anyone. Bullying means being made to do what you don't want to do by means of

Understanding friends

physical or emotional threats. The actions and words of a bully can trample and crash the spirits of a child whose self-worth and identity are at an early stage of development. It is fortunate that most children are resilient and manage to resist such attempts to crush them. They learn to adapt and defend themselves as they grow into adulthood, yet scars remain. Many people carry images of themselves which have been damaged at a vulnerable stage in their development. Below the surface of many apparently successful, popular and well-adjusted adults there is still a frightened child. Winston Churchill thought that his schooldays were the worst days of his life and pleaded with his parents to be allowed to stay at home. He vividly and painfully recalled being bullied and hiding behind a tree to avoid being hit by the cricket balls which were thrown at him. All of us can remember some incidents of bullying, but fortunately schooldays for most people contain many more good events than bad.

Sadly, this is not true for everyone. Anne wanted a friend, a special friend just for her. She had plenty of acquaintances but no real friends. In her mid-twenties this issue became increasingly distressing for Anne, so she came to talk to me. As I listened to her story she seemed exceptionally negative about herself. We discovered that she rarely put anything into a friendship because she thought she had nothing to give. 'No-one really wants me as a friend; I don't like myself so why should anyone else like me?' As we talked about Anne's past she recounted her time at school and suddenly remembered, a painful memory that she had repressed for years, that she had been bullied by an older girl for a whole year. As a result Anne learned that in order to get friends you must fit in and do what others expect of you. She had pushed her feelings of hurt

Making friends with ourselves

and anger deep down within her, where like some underground stream they kept flowing on, pouring out a loathing of herself for being weak. Anne had learnt one way of surviving while she was at school. She defended herself by doing what others wanted at the expense of her own needs and feelings. Now as an adult she was discovering that she did want her needs met, and she wanted a friendship where she could be open and honest about her feelings.

Because Anne felt of little value she did not have a secure base, and friendship became unpredictable, a dream with no basis in reality. Yet as she learned more about herself and the pattern she was living by, she could see that there was the possibility for change. Anne decided that she had had enough 'bullying' and was going to do things for herself instead of always for other people. She began making demands of people as she had never dared before, and to her amazement they began to respond. One day when she came to see me, her whole face was transformed by a smile, as she triumphantly said, 'It works.' There were some ups and downs for Anne, but she came to see that others could value her as a friend—not just because she did what they wanted, but for herself.

If we feel that because of our past we are of little value, we still have the option of standing up to these 'bullying events' and discovering that we are much stronger and have more to offer to others in friendship than we might think.

BEING HURT
Everyone is hurt sometimes, but some people are hurt more than others. Being human means living in a far from perfect world, full of far from perfect people. I believe that one of the most traumatic events which can happen to anyone is to be abused as a child, whether the abuse is physical, sexual

Understanding friends

or psychological. Having worked with Rachel for several years, first as a counsellor and then as a friend, I have seen at first hand the effects of sexual abuse, in terms of negative thinking, shattered trust, distorted affection, red-hot anger and rage, profound rejection, isolation, and a shattered self-image. Obviously anybody who has been abused needs specialized care and counsel. They also need friends, yet feel unable to make any. 'Nobody will believe me', they think to themselves. 'Who would have me for a friend if they knew the real truth?'

There are many traumas that we might experience during our formative years as children. They include such events as the death of a person close to us, separation due to illness, becoming aware that we are scarred or disabled in some way, or discovering we are adopted. However the most common traumatic event which children and young people are likely to face is the divorce of married parents or the separation of parents living together. On average in Britain 436 children every day are affected by the pain of divorce and this number is rising. It seems incredible that we are only now beginning to realize the devastating effect that divorce has on children. The loss of any relationship is usually accompanied by feelings of guilt, bitterness, betrayal and reproach and causes an experience similar to bereavement. In some ways it is worse than bereavement because there is no choice when a person dies. In that case it is a matter of coming to terms with the fact that the dead person will never be there again. However in divorce the lost parent is still around, albeit at a distance. This makes it hard to understand why they would want to leave and more difficult to work through the feelings of grief. Studies suggest that no child is unaffected by their parents' divorce, the most vulnerable being those aged between six and fourteen,

Making friends with ourselves

and it takes at least a year to adjust to the new situation. It may be true that 50 per cent of children show no signs of on-going damage due to the break-up, but this still leaves a very large number of children who are adversely affected. A crucial factor appears to be the absence of a father in the first year of adjustment highlighted by the fact that it is more often the mother who gains custody of children. The greater the time lost with the father, the greater the degree of disturbance in that first year.

Two lasting effects may be seen. Children may blame themselves for the parents' break-up. 'If only I had been a good boy, Mummy would not have gone away.' 'It's all my fault, I must be so horrid that Daddy has to leave.' This of course can have a destructive effect on the way people think and feel about themselves. Ian was the best footballer in the school, and everybody wanted him on their side. He seemed to be everybody's friend, yet when he went away to university he found that he would get into friendships that quickly fizzled out. He became increasingly unhappy with himself, really wanting a close friend but never able to find one. Ian talked to me about this and we explored how he felt about the divorce of his parents when he was nine. It had left him feeling that if he ever was close to anyone again, he would eventually destroy them in the same way in which he had destroyed his parents. Ian began to see that it was he who pushed people away when they wanted to develop a closer friendship with him.

The continued absence of a parent can also distort a person's ability to relate to adults of the same sex as that parent, both as a child and later as an adult. If, for example, a father leaves the marriage, both boys and girls suffer. Girls lose that safe, opposite sex person, who can do so much in helping a growing girl accept her sexuality. But boys lose

Understanding friends

someone who models what being a man is all about, someone who gives approval, man to man. No matter how much approval is given to them by their mother, there is something distinctive about this acceptance by another man. So as the boy becomes a man, he may seek out older men as friends. The Men's Movement in America has discovered the huge need there is in men to be hugged and accepted by their fathers. One participant in a 'wild man' weekend in Dorset reported:

> Even the most hardened cynic would find it impossible not to be moved as one man after another quietly and often in tears addresses a still and hushed audience. Dead fathers, abusive parents, denied paternity rights, the guilt of fathers, the personal traumas read like a litany of men's fears and failures.[10]

Friends can help men discover their masculinity as long as it is understood that they cannot replace a father.

SKELETONS IN THE CUPBOARD
All this goes to show that the past reveals an assortment of skeletons in the cupboard. What do we do with them in the present?

We need first to be willing to recognize that the skeletons are there. As human beings we have a remarkable capacity to believe what we want to believe, even when evidence to the contrary is staring us in the face. In looking at our past, we need not blame our circumstances or other people for our difficulty in forming friendships. We can, however, acknowledge that these events may have had a greater influence than we had thought, or may be connected in some way we had not imagined. We are learning to have a realistic view of ourselves which does not paper over the cracks

Making friends with ourselves

and pretend that everything is fine. This is a step in the right direction towards building a healthy self-image.[11]

Then we can choose to be survivors and refuse to live as victims of the past. Ivan Denisovich is the central character in Alexander Solzhenitsyn's semi-autobiographical novel about life in a Russian labour camp. Charting one day in Ivan Denisovich Shukhov's life, Solzhenitsyn shows clearly that Ivan had become a survivor through an act of will. The book's penultimate paragraph concludes:

> Shukhov went to sleep fully content. He'd had many strokes of luck that day: they hadn't put him in the cells; they hadn't sent the team to the settlement; he'd pinched a bowl of kasha at dinner; the team leader had fixed the rates well; he'd built a wall and enjoyed doing it; he'd smuggled that bit of hacksaw-blade through; he'd earned something from Tsezar in the evening; he'd bought that tobacco. And he hadn't fallen ill. He'd got over it. A day without a dark cloud. Almost a happy day.[12]

Even in the midst of injustice and cruelty there is something indomitable about the human spirit, but there must be that decision, that will to survive. The New Testament shows us the importance of one's will (1 Corinthians 7.37) and of taking personal responsibility for ourselves (Galatians 6.5). When we have fallen victim to other people, we are left with the choice between remaining a perpetual victim, or of moving beyond that to become a survivor. This is no 'stiff upper lip' mentality but a genuine acknowledgement of the hurt in the past and a deliberate choice not to be imprisoned by it. This has important repercussions for our self-image and our ability to reach out in trust again in making friends. It also reflects a biblical understanding. The

Understanding friends

New Testament encourages us as 'new creations' to live in the light of a future hope with the help of friends, the Church and the Holy Spirit.

We can do ourselves tremendous good by giving and receiving forgiveness, especially where those who have hurt us are concerned. The way in which we deal with hurt and the feelings of anger that often result is important. We feel angry about the way we have been treated, used or let down. Sometimes that anger is turned inward and it stockpiles (like emotional high explosive shells) in the armoury of our unconscious. Many Christians are ashamed of feeling angry and do not know what to do about it. Lucy felt depressed and so went to her pastor, who rang me and asked if I would be able to help her. After listening to Lucy, I realized that depression was only the problem on the surface. As with an iceberg, there was a great deal more below the waterline than above. I said that I felt she was a very angry person, which she angrily denied at the time but was soon able to acknowledge. Over the following weeks this subject came up again and again until she felt able to tell me about the cause of her rage. Lucy's depression was clearly caused by her inability to deal with anger; she felt that if she expressed it she would destroy herself and others, and so she had to keep it under control at all costs. But all the time it was burning away inside her like some smouldering fire.[13]

Feelings of hurt and anger also raise the question of forgiveness. On the release of the British hostage Terry Waite, the question of forgiveness was raised by an American missionary whose release from captivity in Iran Terry Waite had helped negotiate. The BBC's foreign affairs editor was quite taken aback by the American's talk of forgiveness and said that if he had been held captive he could not possibly

Making friends with ourselves

forgive those who had imprisoned him. Yet as it turned out Terry Waite shared the missionary's very different views on the matter and saw the paramount need to forgive.

Jesus knew that our need of forgiveness was vital and this is one reason why he went to the cross. In following Jesus, the ongoing place of forgiveness is stressed (Ephesians 1.17; Colossians 1.13–14). Many Christians know the words 'Forgive us this day our trespasses, as we forgive those who trespass against us' (Luke 11.14), yet experience difficulty in forgiving themselves or others. Forgiveness is easy in theory. But when we have been hurt by someone we have to be willing to let go of the hurt, and that is hard to do if we have been clinging on to it for a long time. If we do not let go, bitterness can grow up in our lives. Like some cancer, it gnaws away on the inside, capable of spreading through and destroying our spirits. Forgiveness is not always a once-for-all act. It can be a process of letting go when painful memories are aroused. It is something that we do as an act of will because if we wait until we feel like forgiving someone who has hurt us, we may never do it.

I don't always find it easy to forgive. When I acknowledge that my hurt and anger is stopping me from forgiving others, there are two courses of action that help. The first is to talk to a friend. In fact it is sometimes in talking to a friend that I am helped to discover that I am not making matters better by being unforgiving. The second is to ask for someone to pray with me and for me.

Friends are there to help. It had taken Karen a whole year to begin to tell Jackie what she really felt. Other than her boyfriend and her mother, Karen talked to nobody about herself at any level. So when she had difficulties in these two relationships, there was nobody else around to be a friend. Karen slowly learned the value of friends when it

Understanding friends

comes to dealing with painful issues both in the past and in the present. Even from a somewhat shaky base it is possible to risk, trust, and gain a friend. Simply having someone there, even if they don't have any answers, makes us feel that we are not so awful after all. In time these friends can help us explore the dark recesses of the cupboard where we keep the skeletons.

When I was a boy living in a tenement in Glasgow, we lived in a flat on the top floor. At the bottom of the stairs was a dark, unlit passage way leading out to the close at the back. My twin sister and I used to imagine that all sorts of horrible goings on took place in this passage way. When we came to the bottom of the stairs on the way out to play we would hold hands and rush past as quickly as possible to avoid the 'floating eyes' from getting us. Our mother told us that it was a cat but we never quite believed her! It was a lot easier to face the darkness with a companion than alone. Friends are not a magic answer for everything, but they can help us to face up to and come to terms with the past.

Rachel, whom I mentioned earlier, has been able to accept her painful, abused past by making the choice to become a survivor. She has had to grapple with what it meant to forgive her father and reach out to others in friendship. She wrote this poem for me which I found deeply moving:

> Harbours
> Are safe places
> Stormy-weary vessels
> Need their protection
> For small repairs
> Or—sometimes—
> A complete rebuilding.

Making friends with ourselves

> But ships
> Are built
> For open seas
> And, in time,
> Must lift anchor
> And set sail.

Rachel has discovered that no matter how scarred it may have been, her good self-image allows her to enter into close friendships once more. Her friends are those people able to create safe places for her.

We have seen, then, that past events can influence our ability to make friends. We have also seen that these events can be dealt with sufficiently to enable us to form friendships, and these very friendships in turn can further help bring about healing and acceptance.

5

When friendships fail

The large red London bus pulled out of the side road without stopping. My instant reaction was to stamp on the brakes, and because the road surface was greasy after a shower of rain, I slid into the back of a parked car. Somewhat dazed I climbed out of the car to see the bus disappearing in the distance. I was too shocked even to notice its registration number. I looked at my own car to find the whole front smashed in. The parked car had only a cracked rear light but the bill for the damage done to my car came to £800. What seemed like a minor impact had major economic consequences.

Friendships can be damaged and need repair just like a car. I asked a group of young people in my church what they thought disabled or destroyed friendship. Here is a list of their replies:

— silly arguments which develop into major arguments;
— lack of forgiveness;
— lack of understanding or communication;
— selfishness;
— being two-faced or dishonest;
— lying or deceit;
— gossip;
— pride;
— harsh or sharp words;

When friendships fail

— abusing trust;
— being misled.

This was more than just a theoretical exercise, because I knew of some of the pain behind the replies. It is through give and take, joy and pain, insight and misunderstanding that friends discover how strong or brittle their friendships are. Sometimes friendships need attention if the relationship is not to be damaged. And there are several steps which we can take to help a friendship, instead of simply standing by and allowing things to become worse.

FIRST AID
'Tea for two', I shouted as I walked past the hotel kitchen. My summer job was as a waiter, complete with white coat and bow-tie—much to my friends' amusement. I went back into the dining room to serve another guest, rushed back into the kitchen to place the order, picked up the tea pot and hot water pot and turned to go out of the kitchen. A chip had fallen on the floor and as I unknowingly stepped on it I slipped backwards pouring a pint of boiling hot water over my thigh. The pain was instantaneous and would have been a great deal worse if it had not been for another waiter. Andy was an England under-23 rugby international. With one arm he scooped me from the floor, dashed to a sink, ripped my trousers down and threw a pan of cold water over my leg. His quick thinking and first aid prevented me from being badly scalded.

Friendships need first aid. For many reasons, not least the fact that they are human beings, friends have their ups and downs. We may be moody, unpredictable, hurt, upset, selfish, argumentative, jealous and possessive and it is because we can be like this that small or silly arguments take place.

Understanding friends

When we trust another person in friendship, we are more likely to reveal aspects of ourselves which are less than perfect, and when we are committed to another person, we are more likely to be affected by their reaction to us.

The telephone rang and as I answered it I heard a friend of mine say, 'It's Mike here, how are you doing?' I replied, 'Mike, yes, I think I used to have a friend called Mike, but he's not been in contact for months, in fact I'm not sure he's still alive. Anything could have happened to him and I would be the last to hear.' Why had I responded quite rudely in this way? Mike and I had been friends for years since training at theological college together. We used to see one another when we could, given that our respective churches were miles apart. Circumstances changed in Mike's life and he left the church to work in business, recruiting computer personnel. As he was travelling around the south-east we used to see each other more often. But I suddenly realized that the friendship had become unequal. It always seemed to be me who was taking the initiative in arranging to meet. I became tired of this, feeling that if our friendship were to be worthwhile, Mike should make some kind of effort. What I really wanted to know was whether or not he valued the friendship and whether or not he valued me. Then for four months I never heard a word, even though I knew that there were tremendous changes taking place in his personal circumstances. Because he was a friend, I was able to express my anger to Mike that he seemed to have dropped me from his life. I said that real friendship is a two-way relationship of give and take, and that I felt I had been doing all the giving. Mike understood, and the result of this first aid treatment to our friendship was that it improved and as a result of being more honest with one another about how we felt it moved onto a new level.

When friendships fail

First aid treatment in a friendship requires the recognition that something is not right. There is a risk involved in saying to a friend that there is something wrong. Yet as we have already seen, the ongoing ability to take risks is one of the factors which make friendship the vital thing that it is. Other first aid steps can be the simple willingness to forgive, the clarification of any misunderstanding or breakdown in communication, the recognition that at times we are all selfish and take far more out of a friendship than we are prepared to put in. Each of these factors requires attention so that it can be prevented from doing further, perhaps irreparable, damage. We are human, we do make mistakes, and friends understand that best of all; but having made a mistake we should then do something about it rather than pretend it has not happened. If we begin to hide our feelings from our friends, we start on a long downward slope which creates an increasing distance between us.

TAKING A BREAK
Sometimes friends need to take a break from one another, to have a 'holiday' from the demands and expectations of being a friend. This does not indicate that the friendship is about to fall to pieces, but it does recognize that in the ebb and flow of any close relationship there is a need for space to be separate or alone. If our friendships are in a healthy state, then we do not need to own one another or become totally dependent on one another. Being interdependent allows room for a break. Space to be apart in a friendship, as indeed in marriage, far from doing it any harm, can be an important factor in maintaining that friendship.

There are times too when the demands on us are so great that we lack the energy to put very much into a friendship. We trust that our friend will understand and continue to

Understanding friends

give us the support we need. Real friendship is about coping with ourselves and our friends when life's circumstances make it difficult. It's about failure and misunderstanding, and still continuing as friends. That's what makes friendship such a precious thing—we are accepted even when we are at our worst. A break in a friendship, properly understood, can renew rather than damage the relationship.

DRASTIC REMEDIES

There are times when a friendship requires drastic action if it is to be saved. As I approached the children's ward at the hospital, the ward doors swung wide open and a four-year-old boy came charging out. Wearing nothing but a loose operating gown, he was being chased by several nurses, doctors, and his mother. His mop of blonde hair identified him as Andrew, the very person I had come to see. Eventually Andrew was caught and clung desperately to his mother. He had been given a pre-med to relax him before his operation, but this had obviously had little effect. Outside the children's ward was an attractive wooden rocking horse. Eventually Andrew calmed down and allowed himself to be rocked backwards and forwards. While he was not looking, the anaesthetist appeared and gave him an injection in his bottom. Suitably anaesthetized Andrew had his operation, though if he is ambivalent about horses in future I wouldn't blame him! Drastic problems require drastic solutions.

A friendship can reach the point where some action is crucial in order to prevent its complete breakdown. This means we need to acknowledge how serious the situation is. Our pain at potential rejection sometimes causes us to make excuses for the other person. None of us likes admitting failure, especially when we have put a great deal of time,

When friendships fail

emotion and energy into a friendship but the truth needs to be faced before it can be dealt with. Two of the most common destructive factors are gossip and a breaking of trust.

Sometimes we tell other people things about our friend, which we should have kept to ourselves. The Bible views gossip and its destructive effect in a very serious light. The Epistle of James explains in very stark terms how what we say can potentially be a great help to other people or do enormous harm:

> Consider what a great forest is set on fire by a small spark. The tongue also is a fire, a world of evil among the parts of the body. It corrupts the whole person, sets the whole course of his life on fire, and is itself set on fire by hell (James 3.5b–6).

The gossiping tongue is like a flame starting a full-scale blaze. Over the past few years the south of France has been plagued with fires razing to the ground huge stretches of countryside and claiming the lives of local residents, holidaymakers and fire-fighters, as well as causing untold ecological damage. Most of these fires are started by unextinguished cigarettes dropped by walkers or thrown away by drivers. It seems incredible that so small a glowing ember can wreak such blazing havoc. Similarly, if you have experienced the effects of just a casual word of gossip, you will have your own painful memories. It is difficult to describe that sense of betrayal. Sometimes people we considered to be friends may prove to be two-faced, showing one side of themselves to us and quite another to their other friends. In the different youth groups with whom I have worked there has been at least one crisis every year due to gossip. Close friends split up and other young people take sides.

Understanding friends

To deal effectively with gossip, we need to confront the friend who appears to have offended. Even though we feel upset or angry, it is helpful to find out the facts, without hostility, because there may have been a simple misunderstanding. It might be that our friend has simply made a mistake and is very sorry. He or she may have let something out by accident, and rushing in with accusations won't help. However, there are some people who simply seem unable to stop themselves from interfering. When I was at school I liked a girl called Nicky Brown. As boys and girls do she used to hang around so we would bump into one another. In order to impress a new friend in my youth group, I told him, somewhat big-headedly, that she was following me around. He went and told her this and several days later Nicky gave me a verbal ear-bashing for saying that she had been following me around. I was left in no doubt as to what she thought of me! At first I could not believe that my new friend had done this, but I noticed that he did the same thing to someone else soon afterwards, and needless to say we did not remain friends very long. Gossip destroys friendship and it needs, like a flame on dry ground, to be stamped out quickly.[1]

USING PEOPLE
Exploitation is never pleasant. As tourists on our first visit to Paris we stood gazing at the Eiffel Tower. A photographer approached us and asked if we would like our picture taken. While we were still discussing this he took several polaroid photographs and then demanded a huge amount of money. We felt we had no choice but to pay a large sum of money for four out-of-focus, poor quality photographs. We had been well and truly exploited, as tourists are the world over.

When friendships fail

Sadly, friends also may exploit one another. It can seem that the empathy and care which were once part of the relationship are no longer there. We feel taken for granted. We resent having to make the first move all the time. The trust we have placed in another person is being abused, so what can we do? Often we do nothing because we have no other friends who are quite so close. We fear that if we challenge or confront our friend, we will be left in a worse position. So we repress our true feelings and begin the process of withdrawal. We no longer share quite so much or make so much of an effort. But our feelings often do eventually emerge, not so much in what we say but in how we say it. Our bodies, tone of voice and the various non-verbal means of expression which we have seen to be important in forming friendships, betray what we really feel. This in turn may result in communication difficulties and misunderstandings which cause us to withdraw even further. Unless we decide to take action the friendship will fail.

It is often when we are trying to rescue it, that we discover how much a particular friendship means to us. Sometimes we realize too late, to our cost, how we have exploited a friendship. We see clearly how we have devalued another person through betraying a confidence or by gossip. Norah always relied on Diane's friendship. They had been best friends all the way through school until Norah discovered boys. Being the better looking of the two she always had a boy in tow. Yet when the relationship broke up, it was always Diane she turned to for support. Their friendship would be back in full swing until a new boyfriend arrived on the scene. When Diane went to university, away from the shadow of her vivacious friend, she discovered that people liked her. They wanted to be her friend and didn't relegate her to second best, boyfriend or no boyfriend. Norah, still at

Understanding friends

home, discovered how lonely it was to be without a girlfriend. It dawned on her that she had exploited the friendship, using Diane's care when it was convenient. Sadly, Norah learned this too late, as she and Diane drifted apart, but she never forgot it in future friendships.

Even if the friendship never recovers, we still have an important obligation to go and ask forgiveness for making use of people. If we are tempted to say it was as much their fault as ours, then perhaps our pride needs dealing with too. Through asking forgiveness we will help the person whom we have hurt to feel valued, and help ourselves to accept that our actions have consequences which must be faced.

BREAKING UP
For a minister, moving from one church to another is a traumatic process. A friend of mine helped me by suggesting that it was like a bereavement: I had to let go of all those lives in which I had been involved. It was no longer 'my' church, if it had ever truly been that in the first place. It took me two years to get over it. Then gradually I felt I could start to put down roots once more and the new place where I was living and working began to feel like home.

When a significant friendship comes to an end there are similar feelings. Friends now friendless may experience shock and disbelief. Even though the friendship may have been foundering for some time and a certain emotional distancing has taken place, it is still a shock when it becomes clear that the relationship has ended. There may simply be an unaccountable feeling of general sadness until we realize that a particular friend is no longer around. The shock may also express itself in the form of a paralysing numbness into which we retreat after the loss of any close relationship. The loss of a friend may be a great shock, or it

When friendships fail

may seem to pass quite smoothly. If the latter is the case, it may raise questions about how much we put into the relationship in the first place.

As the shock recedes, it brings in its wake a variety of feelings which express the emotional pain. Feelings of betrayal, brokenness and a crushing sadness may dominate our thinking. At this stage people often discover afresh the biblical accounts of Jesus in Gethsemane (Matthew 26.36f.) and his cry of dereliction, 'My God, my God, why have you forsaken me' (Matthew 27.45). I remember a colleague describing his pain when he introduced his wife to a close friend of his. At college this person had been his best friend, although because their spheres of work were different they had not seen each other for some time. There was sadness in his voice when he said that after spending a few minutes with him and his wife his old friend went off to talk to a whole crowd of other people instead. Clearly for Jim's friend the relationship had died and meant nothing more than a few moments' happy reminiscing. For Jim the relationship was still at the painful stage—he had probably been unaware that the friendship was over until this meeting took place.

Sometimes these feelings are expressed in anger, which if it is not dealt with often resurfaces as depression.[2] If this anger is turned inward, it may significantly hinder the formation of other friendships. If someone feels that the end of the friendship was all his or her fault, this confirms to them what a rotten person he or she is. Then it may seem that the only safe way of avoiding this type of pain is to prevent others from getting close again. But this downward spiral takes us right back to stage one. It's like a game of snakes and ladders. Near the top of the board there is a square containing the longest snake on the board which leads back

Understanding friends

to the bottom of the board again. Just when we think we have won the game of friendship it may seem that we are back at the bottom of the pile once more. We can either get depressed about this and, like children in the playground, say we are not going to play any more; or we can decide that it will take us too long to get back up again by searching for the right ladders. Other friends may be there to help with these ups and downs. Either way, a time will probably come when we want to make a fresh attempt at this risky and life-affirming business of friendship.

Friendships may fail, but there are steps we can take to help ourselves and others. We can both give and receive first aid, that immediate attention which stops the rot setting in. It may be that we need a break from a friendship to allow us some breathing space, so that when we return to the friendship it may be renewed and become significant again. Drastic action is sometimes necessary to rescue a friendship which we value, and whether we succeed may depend on our ability to give or receive forgiveness. Finally, there are times when, either because of circumstances beyond our control or for the good of future friendships, we must let go of past memories and recognize that a particular friendship is no more.

6

Obstacles to friendship

It was a sad day when Andrew and Mary discovered they couldn't have children. As they slowly came to terms with their loss, they decided to explore the possibility of adopting a child. They had connections in Romania and so they hoped they might be able to adopt a Romanian child. Initially the authorities were very helpful but the couple soon found themselves embroiled in a bureaucratic nightmare. One obstacle followed another as they pursued their dream of adoption. Friendship, too, poses a number of obstacles to be overcome, before the full potential is developed. There are a number of things which may halt our progress during the growth of a friendship, including fantasy, the physical expression of friendship, time, and marriage.

FANTASY
All of us have dreams. We may dream of running in the Olympics, appearing on TV, being stunningly good-looking, preaching to thousands, writing a best-seller, or driving a Ferrari. The list is endless. Most of the time we accept that we will never do these things. Yet fantasy may play a major part in hindering our development as people and our friendships. We fantasize about many things, but there are some that are more harmful to developing friendships than others. Men, more than women, escape into the fantasy of pornography, and women, more than men,

Understanding friends

escape into the fantasy of romance. Both men and women escape from the drudgery or pain of living through the characters in soap operas. All these forms of fantasy may attack the very foundations of friendship.

Pictures of naked women have a strong appeal to men. Part of this is instinctual, but we do not always have to indulge our instincts. In chapter two we saw how sexual appetites are used to sell products. Such sales techniques debase the unique way God has made us as physically male and female. This is especially the case in pornography. Magazine after pornographic magazine reveals the ideal woman to be slim, large breasted, perfectly sun-tanned, with legs apart in availability. Women are portrayed not as individuals but as glossy pin-ups to be stared at and fantasized over, while on the cinema screen they come complete with moans and groans. The reaction of some people to this is to say things like, 'It's just a bit of fun'; 'It's not as if it's "hard porn" or anything serious'; and 'Everybody does it, you can't expect people to be puritanical these days.'

The findings of an American commission researching pornography, however, published in a book called *Pornography: A Human Tragedy*, suggest otherwise. The book revealed that exposure to milder forms of pornography led people to desire more bizarre kinds. After exposure to only six hours of non-violent sexual videos people came to believe the following:

— the greatest sexual joy comes without on-going commitment;
— partners expect each other to be unfaithful;
— there are health risks in repressing sexual urges;
— promiscuity is natural.

A follow-up study recorded the following repercussions:

Obstacles to friendship

— diminished satisfaction with the physical appearance of one's partner;
— reduced satisfaction with the partner's sexual behaviour;
— greater importance attached to sex without emotional involvement.[1]

Pornography is a retreat into a fantasy world which can rob people of true friendship. There is no risk-taking, there is no tentative reaching out to another, and there is no facing the reality that friends make demands. Friends demand that we give something of ourselves and it is this give and take process that prevents friends from exploiting one another.

One insidious aspect of the hugely lucrative pornographic trade is that it exploits not only women but also the real and widespread hunger for relationship and friendship. In a television series *Sex Now*, a number of diaries were kept and quoted anonymously on the programme. One young man wrote this: 'Today I watched a porno movie. Maybe it's because I have not got a girlfriend.' What he discovered was that once he had a girlfriend he didn't need the 'porn and the fantasy' any more. Describing the incredible pleasure brought by a kiss he discovered there is no comparison between a celluloid image offering everything on a television screen and a real, living relationship offering a single kiss. Pornography is like an expensively wrapped present with nothing inside, and the tragedy is that people settle for the shiny paper instead of the real thing. Friendship is the real thing that people want, though it's not readily available like a neat package on the shelf.[2]

In romantic pulp fiction there are stereotyped characters holding out the fantasy that the woman always gets her man despite the trials of true love. There is always a happy

Understanding friends

ending, and teenage girls, bored housewives and others escape into this idealized picture of relationships. As far as I know nobody has conducted any research into whether this fantasy does harm in the way pornography obviously does—but it is certainly an escape from, or a substitute for, real relationships and real friendships. Curling up with a romantic novel is not a lasting cure for loneliness. It may meet an immediate need, like a bar of chocolate in the middle of the afternoon, staving off the hunger pangs until tea time. But neither chocolate nor the fantasy of the romantic novel is a substitute for the real thing.

Julie was a tall, attractive blonde. She had always been good-looking and her mother had instilled into her the notion that she would be able to take her pick of available men. Her mother had a romantic, fantasy-type understanding of relationships, and believed that her daughter would naturally attract a tall, dark, handsome partner, preferably someone who was sporting as well. Julie grew up viewing people superficially. She did become involved with a tall, dark, handsome man and he treated her appallingly. Her mother could see only good in him. In the end Julie left him and started a relationship with someone quite opposite in looks, but who was gentle and caring. Their relationship has proved to be both lasting and truly happy, but her mother still thinks she settled for second best. A stereotyped view of other people can be a real hindrance in being able to form friendships. We can become so preoccupied with a fantasy of what a 'perfect' friend is, that it prevents us from ever getting close enough to others to see that friendship is a great deal more complicated and a lot more rewarding than the fantasy.

Angie was a barmaid at the Queen Victoria Pub, known to all as the 'Queen Vic'. Unhappily married and a heavy

Obstacles to friendship

drinker, she attempted suicide. Angie is a fictional character in the English television soap, *EastEnders*. After her televised overdose, the casualty departments of several hospitals admitted women of a similar age and background who had also tried to commit suicide. This could be a coincidence but for some people it seems that the drama had become so real it was no longer entertainment. The lonely, unhappy and friendless Angie summed up the despair of their own lives. The dividing line between fact and fiction is very narrow. On the one hand, soaps can be enjoyable entertainment. They appeal to the nosey side of our nature and deal with everyday dramas with which we can identify. But they can also lead to a vicarious living out of other people's lives. The characters act and react as we would like to but are afraid to. They can almost become a substitute for friends, because it is easier to make 'friends' with a character on a television series than to go through the process of risking and trusting that friendship requires. After all there is no possibility of rejection. We can soon forget that these 'friends' are actors playing a part, and that what we really need are friends who will refuse to join in the play-acting and help us to face real life.

PHYSICAL EXPRESSIONS OF FRIENDSHIP
Another obstacle in friendships is touch. We saw in an earlier chapter the importance of sexuality in friendship. Accepting that we are sexual beings and find others attractive is an important first step in owning that God has made us this way, therefore we should be proud that we think and feel and love. The whole issue of sexuality and sexual relationships has sadly been kept under wraps in the church for many years. So Christians who, for example, commit adultery, simply disappear, and the local church 'hushes the

Understanding friends

situation up'. When this happened in a church where I was a minister, we decided to deal with the issue in the open. The people concerned expressed their repentance to God, said they were sorry to the church, and asked for forgiveness. They also asked for help and understanding as they rebuilt their separate lives. None of this was easy—and the consequences of sin left scars in the lives of many. But it was an important step in the church's recognition that sexuality is important both when it is expressed rightly and when it is abused.

P.D. James, the celebrated crime novelist, touches on the subject of sexuality through one of her central characters, Commander Adam Dalgleish. She describes what Adam is thinking about a female colleague, Inspector Kate Miskin:

> It would have been dishonest to say that there was no hint of sexuality between them. In his experience there nearly always was, however repudiated or unacknowledged, between any reasonably attractive heterosexual couple who worked closely together. He wouldn't have chosen her if he found her disturbingly attractive, but the attraction was there and he wasn't immune to it. But despite this pinprick of sexuality, perhaps because of it, he found her surprisingly restful to work with.[3]

An acknowledgment of sexuality is important outside the world of fiction in all our relationships, if we are to see them as they truly are. At this point it is important to draw a distinction between sexuality, the capacity for intimate relationship, and what I want to call physicality, the expression of our sexuality in physical ways. Unless we face the issues of our own sexuality and the limits we choose to place on the physical expression of our feelings for someone else, there will always be obstacles in our friendships. The way

Obstacles to friendship

we relate physically to other people can send them either positive or negative messages.

Touch can communicate acceptance. I once visited an elderly lady who knew she was dying. As she lay in her hospital bed, I held her hand to pray with her. Conscious of her own weakness she said, 'It's nice to hold such a safe, strong, warm hand.' As a single lady she had no family, all her relatives had already died and she had very few friends. The simple act of holding her hand meant so much to her. It showed that she was not alone, that someone was willing to reach out, hold her and help her face the arrival of death. On another occasion a telephone call woke me up at 2.00 am. The nurse said that Mrs Jones was not going to live much longer. Despite a fractured wrist I drove to the hospital. Minutes before I arrived, Mrs Jones died. The nurse was in tears, and despite my being a complete stranger she turned and embraced me. Through her tears she talked of the sadness she felt that people should ever have to die alone. At that moment she needed to be held, to be in actual physical touch with another living human being.

Jesus understood this so clearly when he touched lepers. Bearing a stigma similar to that carried by Aids sufferers today, they were isolated from ordinary human contact. The only people they could touch were others with the same disease. To be touched, held, hugged, kissed, to have a hand held, are all taken to mean acceptance and care. In certain circumstances, as we have seen, we may not even know the person very well. How much more, then, do we appreciate the touch of a friend.

So if you have lots of single Christian friends, you may assume that many of them are struggling with sexuality. And they will until they get pretty advanced in years.

Understanding friends

> Try giving them hugs: one of the problems with being celibate is that you do without being touched. I tend to go to churches where hugs are socially acceptable, and that has been a real life-saver in recent years.[4]

In our friendships we will discover what level of physical contact is appropriate. An Australian rugby player made this amusing observation:

> Put 10 Anglo-Saxon rugby players on a 10-metre bench and they will instinctively place themselves with a metre space for each with no one touching anyone else. Put 10 French players on the bench and they will sit exactly as they land, draped all over each other at random. And a hand resting on another's knee causes no offence.[5]

The British may be less rather than more comfortable with the touch of others, but it can be an important part of friendship. The touch of a friend brings the security of being physically accepted by another person.

Touch can also be used to communicate sexual or erotic feelings. I held Kim's head and gently stroked it and in some circumstances this would have been construed as more than an affectionate act. Kim was in the midst of an incredibly painful process of grief. I was stroking her head as she held her baby who had died and as she was held by her partner. What is the difference between this stroking, and other forms of skin to skin contact which are often a prelude to sexual intercourse? The difference is the matter of intent, although that intent needs to be found in both people. With a desire for a sexual relationship even the most innocent handshake can become erotically charged. Jesus saw this clearly when he said, 'You have heard that it was said,

Obstacles to friendship

"Do not commit adultery." But I tell you that anyone who looks at a woman lustfully has already committed adultery with her in his heart' (Matthew 5.27–28).

It is not merely a question of laying down a certain level of physical contact as being acceptable between friends of the same or the opposite sex. We know, if we are being honest with ourselves, that there are times when our intent is not what it should be. Adultery in the heart tends to precede adultery in practice. The title of a chapter in a book I read about friendship seemed so innocent; all it said was, 'When Friends become Lovers' but behind this simple title lies untold trauma and pain. In this broken world it does happen and even Christians are not immune; but I believe it destroys the very basis of friendship and can set up sexual encounter as a god. C.S. Lewis puts it this way:

> Nothing is less like a friendship than a love-affair. Lovers are always talking to one another about their love; friends hardly ever about their friendship. Lovers are normally face to face, absorbed in each other; friends side by side, absorbed in their common interest. Above all, Eros (while it lasts) is necessarily between the two only. But two, far from being the necessary number for friendship, is not even the best . . . . Two friends delight to be joined by a third, and three by a fourth.[6]

It may be that we are involved in a friendship which includes a powerful erotic component. Being honest with ourselves is an important start. Limiting the physical expression of that relationship is a next step. Adjusting to a new level of friendship or facing the reality that the friendship might not last is an important and painful third step.

Understanding friends

FINDING TIME

In relationships with our friends another obstacle is that of time. For the actor Burt Reynolds, friends are 'those people I can ring at 2.00 am in the morning'. Since 1976, chat-show host Oprah Winfrey has 'talked every day on the phone to my best girlfriend, Gayle, in Connecticut. We talk for hours about nothing of any significance to anyone on this planet.' Liza Minelli and her best friend spend so much time together that she jokingly says they have a black belt in shopping. Time is vital for friendship, yet it seems to be in short supply. There is a world of difference between a meal in a fast-food burger bar and a meal in a restaurant. Both meet the need of hunger, but one does so in a much more enjoyable way than the other. One tends not to linger in a burger bar; it is not the sort of place to which one goes in order to spend time reminiscing with a friend.

One of our problems is that we sometimes treat friends in the same way as we treat fast food. Friends become a source of maximum convenience and minimum effort. Ajith Fernando in his book, *Reclaiming Friendship*, reminds us of the importance of time in friendship:

> One of the keys to a deep friendship is time spent in long conversation. This is the type of relationship that Jesus had with his friends, the disciples . . . we don't know what it is to spend long periods of conversation with friends . . . People who make the sacrifice of letting long conversation time eat into their schedules—and that is a sacrifice—will know the joy of minds meeting on a deeper level. From this, deep relationships of true friendship will be forged. Jesus was willing to make that sacrifice.[7]

Churches sometimes make matters worse by the amount of time they demand of their members. Because not everyone

Obstacles to friendship

in the church puts a great deal of commitment into its life the demands fall on the same people time and time again. The people who suffer most are their friends. We may become so busy in the church that we do not have time to spend with friends any more. Sooner or later they get the message, and slowly but surely they drop away. Often Christians have no friends outside the church which is a disaster for the evangelistic role of the church. Our friends, the very people who should notice something different about us as Christians, may become the most neglected. Given the time pressures we all face, a careful selection of priorities with friends high on the list is essential.

MARRIAGE
Marriage is another obstacle placed in the way of friendships. People the whole world over rue the day on which their best friend met his or her future partner. Of course there is a sense of happiness for one's friend, but there is also a nagging fear that this is the start of a slow drift in the relationship which will eventually leave one abandoned. The so-called friend may sail off into the sunset with Mr or Mrs Right. The feelings of being dropped or of being second best are not pleasant. A married couple, with all the new demands on them, can become very inward-looking, and it is their friends who suffer initially. A marriage partner may demand a great deal, if not all, of one's time. Sometimes a person may feel insecure about his or her partner being a friend to someone else, whether male or female. The possessiveness that results has an adverse effect on friendship, and if it is established early in a marriage it can become a pattern that robs many people of friendship altogether.

Some of the people who suffer most are those who are single. If they are not dropped completely by their friend,

Understanding friends

they may become marginalized, getting pushed to one side to make room for the friend's marriage partner. Sometimes single people's friendships die a slow, lingering death as one by one their friends, now married, give them less and less time and affection. As a consequence, married people can and should make a concerted effort to form and maintain other friendships. This will enable them to see their marriage through the eyes of others, bringing a fresh perspective on the inevitable ups and downs of married life. Friends may greatly enrich a marriage, but in order to do so, they too need time and attention.

There are, of course, many other things that affect our ability to make friends. Joanne started work in a new office and found one of the other typists very friendly and helpful. Within a month, however, she discovered that she was being used by this so-called friend whose only interest was in getting on with her career. When her 'friend' had to choose between supporting Joanne or siding with the office manager, Joanne was dropped like a hot potato.

Derek was a car salesman who found it very difficult to make friends. He discovered that because in his job he was so used to 'making friends' with a potential customer, his view of friendship had become shallow and transitory.

The list of obstacles could go on and on, and include racism, the pursuit of money, possessions, power and so on, but by facing up to those highlighted here we can continue to be a good friend to others and allow others to be good friends to us.

7

The transforming friendship

As I stood in the cathedral I experienced a sense of solitude and also wonder that people had worshipped for centuries in this place. I gazed at the delicately crafted carvings in wood and stone, the intricately painted ceiling and the technicolour stained glass windows directing rainbow patterned light on to drab stone. I also experienced a sadness that God, who should be so close in this place, seemed so far away. Personally, I found that I could not worship the awesome and remote God witnessed to by this building. Sometimes I have a similar trouble with theology; that, like a cathedral, it can make Jesus so remote.

Jürgen Moltmann, a German Christian theologian, has pointed out the danger of our theological descriptions of Jesus creating a distance between Jesus and ourselves. Moltmann suggests that a good title for Jesus, and one that shows us his love, care and humanity, is that of 'Friend':

> In the notion of Jesus' friendship we find . . . Jesus becomes the friend of sinners and tax collectors; as high priest he sacrifices himself for the life and salvation of others and consummates his love through his death in friendship; as the exalted lord, he liberates men and women from servitude and makes them friends of God.[1]

Jesus demonstrates how he is a friend to people in a variety of ways. In a unique way, he himself can be a friend to

Understanding friends

people who are alienated from God. When he was born he was given the title 'Immanuel', meaning 'God with us', and he was given the name Jesus, meaning 'the Lord saves'. When he was called 'the friend of sinners' the Pharisees could not have chosen a more apt phrase to describe what Jesus had come to do, to save people from their sins. Yet in order to do this Jesus needed friends himself. He chose twelve men to follow him as his disciples, with whom he developed particular friendships. Even among the disciples Jesus appears to have chosen three, Peter, James and John, with whom he enjoyed a closer and deeper friendship.

JESUS'S NEED FOR FRIENDS

For Jesus to be truly our friend he had to be truly like us, and if he was truly like us, then like any other human being he needed friends. As a twelve-year-old boy he went on holiday with his family and their friends. When his mother and father could not find him, they assumed that he was with other members of their large family, playing with his cousins or his friends. It was only when they had not seen him for three days that they began to get worried and eventually discovered that he was still in Jerusalem. Luke records in an enigmatic phrase that 'Jesus grew in wisdom, and stature, and in favour with God and men' (Luke 2.52). Does that mean he had friends? I think it does. When God declared from heaven at Jesus's baptism, 'You are my Son, whom I love; with you I am well pleased' (Luke 3.22), was there a part in the Father's heart that hoped his son would make friends? No father could want anything less for his son.

How important friends were to Jesus can be seen if we ask the question, 'Did Jesus know he was God?' The answer is both 'yes' and 'no'. He knew he was different: his birth had made sure of that. He demonstrated a piercing intelligence

The transforming friendship

beyond his years as a boy; one of the guests at his baptism was Almighty God; and Jesus was aware that he had a special relationship with God his Father. On one hand the life of Jesus shows that he was aware of being divine. But on the other hand, as a real human being, he had to discover for himself who he was and what he was like. And that growth of understanding in anyone's make-up is helped by their friends.

Many people—the rich, the poor, the abused, the rejected, the prostitutes, the foreigners and crowds of ordinary people—wanted to see Jesus, meet him and know him. Part of the attraction of Jesus for these people (an attraction which we too can experience in reading the pages of the gospels) is that he is someone who seems so real. He shows us what each one of us longs to be, and holds out the promise that a friendship with him can produce the most satisfying and fulfilled life imaginable (John 10.10). Jesus needed friends because his was a genuine humanity, and he also shows us how attractive true friendship can be.

JESUS: FRIEND OF SINNERS
Jesus was called the 'friend of sinners' (Matthew 11.9, Luke 7.34), but this was not meant as a compliment. In using this abusive term, the jealous religious leaders were mocking him and suggesting that because he was keeping company with the riff-raff he should not be taken seriously. Yet because Jesus was a 'friend of sinners', and the Bible's verdict is that 'all have sinned', anyone can be Jesus's friend. The main purpose of Jesus coming to this earth as the Son of God was to enable us to be friends with God once more. As we saw in chapter two, God has made us with a capacity for intimate relationship, the most important relationship being with himself.

Understanding friends

What stops us from experiencing this friendship with God? Think for a moment about those factors which damage or destroy friendship, that we explored in chapter five: a lack of understanding or breakdown in communication; selfishness; being two-faced or dishonest; lying or deceit; pride; and abusing trust. All these can be applied to our relationship with God, and as a consequence we are alienated and estranged from God. Amazingly he still wants us as friends, even though we have proved to be so difficult. Until we are honest enough to admit that there are huge problems between us and God, and until we face up to the pride which insists that we can sort this problem out on our own, we will always miss out on God's friendship, both now and in eternity. Jesus was the friend of sinners 2,000 years ago and he is still the friend of sinners today.

DISCIPLES BECOME FRIENDS
We know from the gospels that Jesus wanted a small group of people to follow him, even if it meant leaving their jobs or their families behind. With these disciples, Jesus embarked on the greatest rescue mission the world has ever seen. They were to become his closest friends. He shared himself completely with them and they became 'the companions of his human heart: those to whom his affections turned in purely human attachment. His heart was open and readily responded to the delights of human association, and bound itself to others in a happy fellowship.'[2]

It is fashionable today to talk of making our own 'space', where we can be free from pressures and responsibilities. My 'space' is listening to music, which is often very loud, and this is possible only when there is no-one else in the house. Jesus had no such 'space'. The communal lifestyle of first-century Palestine meant that Jesus spent most of his

The transforming friendship

twenty-four hours in the day, seven days a week, with his disciples, apart from the times he went off on his own to pray.

When you spend a great deal of time with someone, you soon learn what kind of person they are. During a week when several students and I were working with a local church, I shared a bedroom with a friend of mine. As the week went on, the friendship became a little strained by the volume of his snoring. I would lie there at night, tired, wanting to go to sleep but prevented by his imitation of a jumbo jet. Our sharing of the good news of Jesus with others meant that I had to share in my friend's snoring. I doubt if Jesus had that problem, as on one occasion he was able to sleep soundly through a howling gale; but sharing everything with his disciples was the foundation of their friendship. On one occasion, Jesus said to them, 'I called you friends, for everything that I have learned from my Father I have made known to you.' (John 15.15). As we examine the relationship between Jesus and his friends we can learn more about our friendship with Jesus. Among the things Jesus shared with his disciples were his ideas, his own character, his feelings and his love.

According to Matthew's account of Jesus's teaching, Jesus proposed a radical new understanding of friendship. 'You have heard it was said "Love your neighbours [whether they be friend or foe[3]], and hate your enemy." But I tell you: Love your enemies' (Matthew 5.43–4). I wonder if Jesus tried his stories out on the disciples first. On several occasions he certainly had to explain them to the disciples, so that the truth he was teaching would sink in. In fact Jesus shared more than simply his ideas with the disciples; he also talked to them about his death. Often they did not understand the significance of these references, yet Jesus, as part

Understanding friends

of his relationship with his friends, did not hold anything back. Afterwards they would no doubt have been annoyed with themselves when they thought back and understood what Jesus had said. They were the first people to know. Having a group around him to encourage him, travel with him, give him moral support, organize the crowds, find food and somewhere to stay, all helped Jesus to communicate the most profound ideas this world has ever known.

Jesus also shared his character with the disciples. As they listened to Jesus's teaching and saw how he lived, the disciples would have come to understand something of his unique character. One day Jesus asked them this question: 'Who do people say I am? . . . . What about you . . . who do you say I am?' (Mark 8.27, 29). Peter's reply shows that he had at last begun to understand the real character of Jesus, the Messiah. To underline the importance of this understanding, six days later, Jesus took the three disciples who were his closest friends, Peter, James and John, on a special day out. They went up a mountain and before their eyes Jesus was shown as he is normally seen in heaven. They were in the presence of God himself and no wonder they were frightened. The disciples, privileged as they were in being regarded by Jesus as his friends, also knew from these glimpses of his divine nature that they were never his equal. Their friendship was real, but of a different order from that, for example, of David and Jonathan.

Then Jesus also shared his feelings and emotions with the disciples. He does not appear to have hidden any feeling or emotion. Not for him the stoical, stiff upper lip approach. He was not one of the 'Don't cry, be a brave soldier for mummy' brigade. Jesus felt for those whose lives had been blighted by disease, demonic powers, or death. In the many accounts of his compassion, Jesus expressed his feelings in

The transforming friendship

sighs, groaning, expressions of anger, rage, indignation and tears. How anyone who had read the gospels could ever have written the hymn 'Gentle Jesus meek and mild' is beyond my comprehension. In Jesus there is raw, stark, humanity at its emotional best.

Above all, Jesus shared his love with his disciples and his friends. One of the most emotional moments described in the gospels is the death of Lazarus. Confronted by the grieving sisters Mary and Martha, we see Jesus reduced to tears. The crowds saw clearly the depth of Jesus's feeling and said, 'See how he loved him!' (John 11.36). Jesus also expressed love in 'the affection which binds man to man in the ties of friendship . . . his heart knit itself to theirs in a simple human fondness. The term employed to express this friendship . . . designates a love that is grounded in admiration and fulfils itself in esteem.'[4] In the last week before his death Jesus told the disciples, 'As the Father has loved me so have I loved you . . . My command is this: Love each other as I have loved you. Greater love has no one than this, that one lay down his life for his friends. You are my friends' (John 15.9, 12–13).

John, who had a special place among the disciples, modestly includes himself in his account of Jesus as 'the one that Jesus loved'. Jesus had just shown the disciples that true power lay not in holding to rank, position or privilege but in serving others. After performing the menial task of washing a guest's feet, Jesus makes a startling pronouncement 'one of you is going to betray me' (John 13.21). Don Carson describes it this way:

> The atmosphere instantly became stultifying again. The silence returned, an engulfing blanket, as the disciples stared at each other. This time there was no doubt what

Understanding friends

the Master meant. The only question was which disciple Jesus had in mind. The stares around the low table were mixed: some curious, some blank, some frightened. Eating came to a standstill . . . . Peter recovered first; but remembering how his last outburst earned him a rather sharp rebuke, he was loath to plunge ahead with the obvious question. He caught John's eye and mouthed a question . . . nodding towards John who lay on the pallet next to Jesus. John leaning on his left arm, slowly twisted backwards so he could talk to Jesus. John's head fell back on Jesus's breast; and then John asked quietly 'Lord who is it?' . . . Everyone stared at Jesus. No-one spoke. Slowly Jesus . . . held out the bread to Judas Iscariot.[5]

That touching moment of intimacy in Jesus's love for one particular disciple, and for the disciples in general, becomes the scene for the enactment of betrayal that was to lead to his ultimate demonstration of love, his death on a cross. What was the reason for this death? Among many important things it accomplished it allowed the whole human race to be friends of God once more (see Romans 5.10–11, Colossians 1.22).

As we have explored friendship in this book, we have seen our crying need for friends in today's world. This is not surprising because that is the way God has made us, to enrich our lives and the lives of others. However, because of the broken nature of our world, there are lessons we need to learn in how we make friends, how we deal with past influences that may impair our ability to make friends, how we maintain friendships, and how we cope when they come to an end. We have examined some of the obstacles that block the path to friendship. Finally, we have looked at the

The transforming friendship

possibility of a transforming friendship with Jesus Christ. This is not a substitute for other friends: his friendship is of a different order. But it adds a new dimension to other friendships; and as we grow in our friendship with Jesus, it will transform our lives and enrich the lives of others, especially our friends.

Notes

1 AN ENDANGERED SPECIES
1. C.S. Lewis, *The Four Loves* (Geoffrey Bles 1960), p. 69f.
2. *The Sunday Times*, 21 April 1991.
3. Jeffrey Masson, *Final Analysis* (Harper Collins 1991), p. 211f.
4. Details of Aelred's life can be found in Aelred Squire's book *Aelred of Rievaulx* (SPCK 1969) and a modern application of some of his ideas in Isabel Anders, *The Faces of Friendship* (Cowley 1992) distributed in the UK by SPCK.

2 THE ORIGIN OF FRIENDSHIP
1. Matthew Campbell, 'The Hand of God Strikes Back', *The Sunday Times*, 31 March 1991.
2. John Stott, 'The Glory and the Shame', *Third Way*, Vol. 13 No. 12, December 1990/January 1991, p. 20; *The Contemporary Christian* (IVP 1992), pp. 36–40.
3. The use of the male pronoun is for grammatical convenience. God as Spirit is neither male nor female but demonstrates characteristics that from our perspective are seen as distinctively male and female.
4. James Houston, *In Search of Happiness* (Lion 1990), p. 8.
5. Lewis, *op. cit.*, p. 69f.
6. Robin Skynner and John Cleese, *Families and How to Survive Them* (Methuen 1983) p. 19f.

7 Lucy Irvine, *Castaway* (Victor Gollancz, 1983), p. 134.
8 John Donne, 'Devotions Upon Emergent Occasions XVII' in *Complete Poetry and Selected Prose* (Nonesuch Press 1972).
9 Josephine Klein, *Our Need for Others and its Roots in Infancy* (Tavistock Publications 1987).
10 *Ibid.*, p. 1.
11 *Ibid.*, p. 2.
12 Mary Anne Coate, *Clergy Stress* (SPCK 1989).
13 Steve Shaw and Sue Plater eds, *Dark Glasses. Sex, Poetry, The Media and Quite a Bit Else* (Marc Europe 1987), p. 109.
14 David Field, 'Sexuality', in S. Ferguson and D. Wright eds, *New Dictionary of Theology*, (IVP 1988), p. 637.
15 David Atkinson, *The Message of Genesis 1–11* (IVP 1990), p. 73.
16 *Loc. cit.*
17 Quoted in Shaw and Platter, *op. cit.*, p. 111.

3 MAKING FRIENDS

1 *TV Times*, 8 January 1991, p. 78.
2 *Sunday Times London Magazine*, 24 February 1991, p. 21.
3 Roy McCloughry, 'The last frontier', *Third Way*, Vol. 15 No. 8, October 1990, p. 18. See also his *Men and Masculinity* (Hodder and Stoughton 1992).
4 Dialogue taken from the filmscript of *Shirley Valentine*, based on Willy Russell's play *Shirley Valentine* (Methuen 1988), p. 12f.
5 Rosemary Dinnage, *One to One. The Experience of Psychotherapy* (Viking 1988), p. 22.
6 Quoted in Selwyn Hughes, *A Friend in Need* (Kingsway 1981), p. 49.

Notes

7 Quoted in Joyce Huggett, *Listening to Others* (Hodder and Stoughton 1988), p. 99. Anne Long sensitively and helpfully develops other ideas related to listening in *Listening* (Daybreak DLT 1990).
8 Dinnage, *op. cit.*, p. 33.
9 *Ibid.*, p. 26.
10 See Alice Fryling and others, *Disciplemakers' Handbook* (IVP 1989).

4 MAKING FRIENDS WITH OURSELVES
1 Lyrics taken from Tracy Chapman's album *Crossroads*.
2 Acts 26.4–11; Romans 7.
3 1 Timothy 1.15; Philippians 1.21.
4 Galatians 1.13–16; 2 Corinthians 11.22—12.10.
5 Dorothy Rowe, *The Depression Handbook* (Collins 1991), p. 86.
6 Quoted in Oliver Gillie's report of the 1991 British Psychological Society Conference.
7 Angela Nuestatter, 'Relative Values', *Sunday Times Magazine*, 27 October 1991, p. 13.
8 *Ibid.*, p. 16.
9 Susie Orbach, 'Strife in the family', *The Guardian*, 10 August 1991, p. 8.
10 Andrew Anthony, 'Wild at Heart', *The Guardian*, 17 October 1992, p. 30.
11 For more reflection on this see Phyliss J. Le Peau, *Resources for Caring People* (IVP 1991), pp. 14–17, 46–47 and Anthony Hoekema, *Created in God's Image* (Paternoster 1986), ch. 6 ('The Question of Self-Image').
12 Alexander Solzhenitsyn, *One Day in the Life of Ivan Denisovich* (Penguin Books 1963), p. 142f.
13 A helpful book on this subject is Myra Chave-Jones, *Living with Anger* (Triangle 1992).

Understanding friends

5 WHEN FRIENDSHIPS FAIL

1 For a longer discussion of this see Ajith Fernando, *Reclaiming Friendship* (IVP 1991), p. 111f.
2 For more details about depression see Alistair Ross, *Helping the Depressed* (Kingsway 1990).

6 OBSTACLES TO FRIENDSHIP

1 Quoted in John Court's article 'Pornography' source unknown.
2 A helpful discussion of pornography can be found in Nigel Williams, *False Images* (Kingsway 1991).
3 P.D. James, *A Taste for Death* (Faber and Faber 1986), p. 354.
4 Quoted in *Renewal Magazine*, no. 185, October 1991, p. 32.
5 Stephen Jones, 'The pen is mightier (and crazier) than the scrum', *The Sunday Times*, 4 November 1990.
6 C.S. Lewis, *op. cit.*, p. 73f.
7 Ajith Fernando, *op. cit.*, p. 18.

7 THE TRANSFORMING FRIENDSHIP

1 Jürgen Moltmann, *The Open Church* (SCM Press 1978), p. 61.
2 Benjamin Warfield, *The Person and Work of Christ* (The Presbyterian and Reformed Publishing Company 1950), p. 106.
3 *Ibid.*, p. 105.
4 *Loc. cit.*
5 Don Carson, *Jesus and his Friends* (IVP 1986), p. 13.

All Bible quotations are taken from *The Holy Bible, New International Version* copyright © 1973, 1978, 1984 by the International Bible Society. Published by Hodder and Stoughton.

Also published by
TRIANGLE

LIVING WITH ANGER
by Myra Chave-Jones

Takes a positive view of anger and how it can be used as an important part of our lives

FREE TO FAIL
by Russ Parker

A Christian exploration of the problems many people have with facing up to failure and its place in the spiritual life.

SEVEN FOR A SECRET THAT'S NEVER BEEN TOLD
Healing the wounds of sexual abuse in childhood
by Tracy Hansen

A moving account of a survivor of child sexual abuse working through the trauma induced by the return of repressed memories.

UNWORLD PEOPLE
For anyone who has felt unwanted, unusable, unloved
by Joyce Landorf Heatherley

Shows the growth of hope and faith after rejection, based on the author's own experience.

HOW MANY TIMES CAN YOU SAY GOODBYE?
Living with bereavement
by Jenifer Pardoe

A down-to-earth look at grief, with many everyday stories to give practical insights into what can be done to understand and help in times of bereavement.

BELIEF BEYOND PAIN
by Jenny Francis
Foreword by Richard Bewes

A remarkable insight into one person's physical pain and its effect on her life, faith and relationships.

LOSING AND LIVING
Thoughts on every kind of grieving
By David M Owen

Considers a range of personal losses – from bereavement of family and friends in death to the loss of our own health, youth or job. It includes many apt and revealing quotations which speak directly of the experience of grief.

Triangle
Books
can be obtained from
all good bookshops.
In case of difficulty,
or for a complete list of our books,
contact:
SPCK Mail Order
36 Steep Hill
Lincoln
LN2 1LU
(tel: 0522 527 486)